Charlton Hall, MMFT, LMFT

Starting a Family Therapy Business

Charlton Hall, MMFT, LMFT

Charlton Hall, MMFT, LMFT

Copyright © 2013 Charlton Hall, MMFT, LMFT

All rights reserved. No part of this book may be reproduced without written permission from the author. No warranty is expressed or implied.

To contact Charlton Hall, email chuck@mbft.org.

ISBN-13: 978-1492891512
ISBN-10: 1492891517

Charlton Hall, MMFT, LMFT

ABOUT THIS BOOK

Although there are many books on starting a business, and even some books on starting a therapy or counseling business, there are none that focus specifically on the special considerations of Marriage and Family Therapists thinking of going into private practice for themselves. This book was written to address these considerations. If you are a Marriage and Family Therapist going into private practice for the first time, this book is for you. If you are another type of mental health professional, you will also find much information that will be useful to you in setting up a private practice.

DISCLAIMER

Although every attempt has been made to verify that the information provided in this book is accurate, laws and regulations regarding health care, insurance, and the medical profession frequently change. Be sure to check with your local laws and ethical codes when using the information in this book. When in doubt, consult with your attorney, accountant, or local licensure board. No warranty is expressed or implied.

Contents

1 Is Private Practice for You? 1

2 Types of Business Entity 15

3 Taxes and Licenses 25

4 Insurance Panels 35

5 EAPs and HMOs 55

6 Professional Organizations 63

7 Advertising 81

8 Branding 103

AFTERWORD 113

Appendix A: Private Practice Resources 115

Appendix B: Private Practice Checklist 119

Appendix C: Secretaries of State..121

References 129

ABOUT Charlton Hall, MMFT, LMFT 133

OTHER BOOKS BY CHARLTON HALL 135

Charlton Hall, MMFT, LMFT

1 Is Private Practice for You?

If you are like most mental health professionals, you got into the field because you wanted to make a difference in the world. And if you're like most mental health professionals, you've spent some time working for an agency. I worked at several state agencies myself before finally going into private practice. While employment at a mental health agency might work for many, for some it can be a difficult experience. Here are some of the reasons why:

- Agencies often pay their licensed professionals around $20 to $30 an hour, while billing insurance companies $80 to $120 an hour. The agency pockets the difference.
- Mental health professionals must obtain continuing education in order to keep their licenses current. A growing trend in most agencies is to have their licensed professionals pay the fees for these continuing education courses out of their own pockets.
- Many agencies hire students and interns in the process of getting licensure, but once they obtain a license, they're not given a

promotion or a raise.
- In many state agencies there is little room for promotion or advancement. About the only jobs available are supervisory positions that bring much more responsibility with only a little more pay.
- Mental health education is expensive, and most agency employees find it difficult to pay student loans and make a living on an agency salary.
- Most agency employees have to do their own case management. More paperwork means less time working with your patients.
- Many agencies don't offer benefits like health insurance or retirement plans (although under the Affordable Care Act, if the agency has more than 50 employees, they will be required to provide insurance).
- Many agencies have a particular treatment philosophy that restricts the range of treatments that their counselors can use. This means that if you would like to use an intervention that is outside of the agency's preferred treatment paradigm, the agency's approach is the one that gets implemented.
- Many agencies have caseloads that are so overwhelming that their therapists and counselors don't get to spend enough time with their patients.
- Due to huge caseloads and lack of funding at most agencies, corners are sometimes cut in treatment. Sometimes this corner cutting puts therapists into an ethical gray area where it is difficult to represent the patient's best interests.

If you became a therapist because you wanted to make a difference, but if practicing in an agency feels too restrictive, then private practice may be the right choice for you. To know for sure if you're ready for private practice, read over these questions below and consider the issues they raise. If you feel comfortable with your answers, then private practice could be right for you!

Are you afraid of failure?
Private practice isn't for the timid. It takes a long time to establish yourself as an independent clinician, even if you have a lot of contacts. A good rule of thumb is to have enough in savings to live on for at least two years. Expect to take a loss in your first year. If you break even in your first year, consider yourself extremely lucky. If you're ready to take a loss for the first year or two, and you have confidence in your ability to run a private practice, then you're probably not afraid of failure.

Don't go into private practice if it's your only means of income. This is especially true if you've never been in private practice before. Most people start off part-time in private practice while working elsewhere, before transitioning to full-time private practice. This can be a difficult task to accomplish if your agency has any non-competition clauses in your contract. You might find it helpful to consult with an attorney first if you are in this situation.

Do you lack knowledge about running a business?
My undergraduate degree was in Experimental Psychology. During my Experimental Psychology class, one of the projects needed subjects with Type A personalities. As usual, we went looking for subjects in the freshman psych classes. Unfortunately, we couldn't find enough Type A students for a successful experimental group, so we had to go recruiting among the business majors!

Most psychology, therapy and counseling programs don't offer courses in running a private practice. Those programs that do barely scratch the surface of this complex topic. If you lack knowledge about the business end of private practice, you're not alone. But don't worry, that's the purpose of this book. You'll still need to find as much information as possible about state and local laws and regulations on opening a business, as well as tax law, insurance, and accounting practices. Most of these topics are covered later on in this book, and there is a list of resources in the appendices to help you gain more practice and knowledge in this complex and often confusing area.

Do you know how to get on insurance panels, EAPs, HMOs and other third party providers?
Insurance panels can make or break a private practice just starting out. The days of running a therapy business on a fee-for-service basis are long gone, so any successful private practice is going to need to have some interaction with insurance panels, EAPs, and/or HMOs. The difficulty here is that every insurance panel is different, so you'll have to know the requirements for all of them. It doesn't help that their rules and regulations change frequently, and they're not always willing to share information with providers. A good rule of thumb here is that if you plan to take insurance, expect to spend two hours of time doing paperwork and making phone calls for every one hour of client contact. If you don't mind paying a subscriber

service to do your medical billing for you, then you might be able to avoid some of this time-consuming paperwork. About the only viable alternative to this is to offer your services on a fee-for-service basis using a sliding fee scale. There are very few therapists who have been successful with such a model, and the ones who are have usually been in practice for several years.

Do you understand how to bill for services?
At first it may seem a simple matter to bill for services, especially on a fee-for-service basis. Many just starting out in private practice think that they simply schedule the appointment, do the service, and then the patient writes them a check. But what about no-shows? Do you bill them for not calling to cancel? What if there's an emergency and the patient leaves before the session is over? How do you bill for that? What if there's a court case and you have to spend hours reading court reports, evaluations, and case files? Should you be compensated for your time? What about patients who only want assessments or letters of recommendation for employment or other purposes? These are all questions you will have to consider and have policies for ahead of time.

Another layer of complexity is added by the fact that if you plan to take insurance, each insurance panel has a different billing procedure. These are often complex and difficult to understand, on purpose. The more reasons insurance companies can find to reject a claim, the less money they have to pay out.

Once I attended a seminar on insurance billing. The facilitator stated that if we followed his methods, we should be able to get 80% to 85% return on our billing, meaning that for every dollar we billed to an insurance company, we should expect to get between 80 and 85 cents if we used his billing methods. I raised my hand and naively asked, "You mean we don't get 100% of what we bill the insurance companies?" The entire room full of therapists, all with much more experience in insurance billing than I had at that time, burst out into laughter. Bottom line: Insurance companies aren't in business to pay out money. If you want to get maximum return on your billable hours, prepare to dot every 'I' and cross every 'T.' Either that, or prepare to engage the services of a medical billing company.

Are you comfortable asking clients for money?
As mentioned previously, there aren't a lot of Type A therapists. Consequently, many therapists and counselors feel

uncomfortable asking clients for money. Many also feel uncomfortable asking for what they are worth. Look at it this way: You spent a lot of time and money getting that license, so you have a right to be compensated for it.

If you have a difficult time asking clients for money, then it's probably a good idea to ask for payment before the session begins. That way you don't feel rushed at the end of the session, and your clients will learn to expect to have payment up-front. My personal policy is that if their account is more than three sessions in arrears, they will not be allowed to schedule another appointment until it's caught up. I spell this out in my intake paperwork so that they know ahead of time what the policy is.

Another issue to consider is what will happen if their insurance denies the claim. While some insurance companies will allow you to bill the client for services they don't cover, others will not. You need to know up-front what the client's insurance policy states regarding collecting payment of denied claims. You should also explain to your clients in your intake paperwork that if their insurance company doesn't pay, and if their policy allows it, the client is responsible for payment. Be aware though, that if an insurance company denies payment for any reason, the client is likely to become upset at you, and not the insurance company, should you ask them to write a check for the unpaid balance. The best way to avoid this is to explain up front and in detail what your collections policy is.

Finally, if you just can't bring yourself to ask for money from your clients, you may wish to consider hiring a receptionist. This is an additional expense that is beyond the means of most private practitioners when they are first starting out, but if you cannot ask your patients for money, you won't be in business for long. So it may be a necessary expense to hire a receptionist.

Do you know how to market yourself?
Marketing can make or break any business, and this is especially true of a private practice mental health business. There are hundreds of ways to advertise your practice, and most of them don't work. The good news is that the ones that work the best are relatively inexpensive and easily accomplished. In the chapter on marketing and advertising, we'll look at the advantages and disadvantages of most forms of advertising.

Another issue with marketing is the idea of *branding*. Branding is related to marketing, but not identical to marketing. Your brand is the overall impression people get when they think of your business. Think of your favorite brand of clothing. What sorts of things come to mind when you think of that brand? What are that brand's characteristics that distinguish it from all other brands on the market? Branding is an often-overlooked tool that can be very useful to your business.

The good news about marketing is that your best advertising is word-of-mouth from satisfied customers. The best thing about word-of-mouth advertising is that it costs nothing. The bad news is that you first have to have satisfied customers before you get any word-of-mouth advertising. The chapter on marketing will offer in-depth suggestions on how to go about getting those first clients in the door as inexpensively as possible.

Are you a business or a charity?
Let's face it, you wouldn't have gone into a caring profession if you didn't care about people. Because of the caring nature of therapists, we tend to want to help people. Sometimes those people might not have the money to afford our services. If that's the case, it can be tempting to see them at a reduced rate or on a pro bono basis. While a successful practice can and should provide some of these services to people without the money to pay the full fee, it's difficult to sustain a viable business if more than half of your caseload is paying a reduced fee. If you can't keep the doors to your business open, you can't help anybody.

If you find yourself drawn to helping underserved populations who may not be able to afford your services, then you may wish to consider either joining a nonprofit agency, or starting your own if there isn't one in your area that serves your target population.

Do you know how to seek out referrals?
Knocking on doors is one of the least expensive ways to bring people into your private practice. About the only expenses for this method of advertising are gas money and business cards. It amounts to door-to-door sales, calling on doctors' offices, state and local agencies, and other mental health businesses. The more often they see your face, the more likely they are to remember you and to refer people to you. So if you're shy or hesitant about selling yourself, you're going to have a hard time with this approach. Where many startup private practices fail is in thinking that they only have to seek out referrals once, when

they first open the doors to their practice. The problem with this line of reasoning is that there is a lot of turnover in the health care professions. So if you introduce yourself to the staff at a doctor's office now, the staff may have completely changed six months from now and nobody will know who you are. You will also want to make sure that all your referral sources have up-to-date information and brochures about what current services you might be offering. This is one aspect of marketing that cannot be jobbed out to other people. If you're the one doing the therapy, doctors, therapists, psychiatrists and other referral sources will want to get to know you personally, and not a paid representative of you or your practice. If you're not comfortable with this hands-on approach to seeking referrals, then private practices is probably not for you.

Do you know where to find referrals?
There is a certain amount of bush-beating that goes along with being in private practice. This means that you have to keep up with changes in your community and its resources. Agencies come and go with a fair amount of speed and regularity, and you never know when a new agency might be a referral source. We'll go into more depth into where to find referrals in the chapter on marketing. If you don't know how to do this yet, don't worry. It's a skill that can be learned.

Do you have the support of your family and friends?
If you've never run a business before, going into private practice can be one of the most rewarding, but most stressful, things you've ever done. Does your family support your decision? If the business fails, what will it do to your family's financial situation? Do your friends think you have the skills needed to be a success? It can be very difficult to go into any business venture without the aid of your support group. This is doubly true for starting a private practice therapy business, since you will be dealing with other peoples' problems, in addition to your own, on a regular basis.

It may also help to have a peer support group that meets on a regular basis. I have a group of local therapists who meet for coffee once a month to talk over the trials and tribulations of private practice, and to share ideas. If you choose to start such a group, make sure you set firm boundaries about discussing clinical information so that you don't violate the confidentiality of your patients.

Can you afford the startup costs?
Starting a family therapy business can be deceptively expensive. You may think that all you need to do is rent an office and get a telephone, but there's much more to it than that. There are membership dues to professional organizations. There are continuing education and licensing renewal fees. If you use a paper-based office, there is a fairly large cost associated with the purchase of paper, ink, and printing supplies. There are business licenses, taxes, and advertising fees. A good rule of thumb for determining your startup costs is to think of everything you possibly can, down the last penny, then add 25% for those unforeseen things. Also plan not to turn a profit for at least your first year in business.

If you were able to answer the above questions successfully, then you may well be on your way to starting a successful private practice. In addition to the skills listed above, there are other characteristics that most successful practitioners have in common. Some of these are listed in the next section.

Characteristics needed to start a successful private practice
It goes without saying that if you intend to run a successful private practice family therapy office, you need to be a competent Marriage and Family Therapist, so I'm going to assume that you have graduated from a good COAMFTE-accredited Marriage and Family Therapy program (or other graduate program if you are not a Marriage and Family Therapist) and that you are fully licensed, or well on your way to being fully licensed, and are entitled to legally practice Marriage and Family Therapy in the state where you are considering opening a practice.

In addition to good general clinical skills, you may wish to work with a target population, or a specific model, or a specific diagnosis. Just be aware that specializing can be a two-edged sword. If, for example, you choose to specialize in Borderline Personality Disorder because there are no other therapists in your area who specialize in that diagnosis, then you are likely to get quite a few people with that diagnosis. The drawback to limiting yourself to that specific diagnosis is that only a small percentage of the overall population with need for therapy services would desire or require your particular area of expertise, so you are limiting your referral base from the start. It can be a balancing act to determine whether you would do better to generalize, and therefore insure a larger referral base, or specialize, and get more referrals from therapists who lack skills in your area of expertise.

Whatever you decide, most therapists in private practice share a few skills in common. These skills help them to succeed in the highly competitive world of private practice mental health. Some of these skills include:

A Passion for the Profession
Do you truly have a passion to be a successful private practice family therapist? People don't go into this line of work to get rich. We enter this profession because we care about other people and want to help. Now is the time for soul-searching honesty. If you are 100% certain that you can sustain your enthusiasm in the private practice profession over an extended period of time, then you're ready for private practice. But if you go into it with a 'guess so' approach, you're destined for failure. The most successful people in this profession are those who are passionate about what they do for a living. Your chances of striking it rich in this profession are about the same as your chances of becoming a rock star overnight, so if money is your primary motivation, you're in the wrong profession. Private practice is for those who truly love the profession of helping people. Only people who do it for the love of doing it stay in this business long-term.

Persistence
Some would call this 'stubbornness.' Others might call it, 'tenacity.' However you choose to label it, persistence is a necessary quality for those who make it in private practice. This is not a profession for those who give up after the first try. You're going to make mistakes. Some of those mistakes are going to be painful. You can minimize them by learning as much as possible before going into business for yourself, but I've yet to meet anybody in this profession who hasn't run across at least a few stumbling blocks.

If you're certain that you have a passion for this profession, the next step is to clarify your goals. What do you hope to achieve with your private practice? How are you going to do it? What is your business plan, and how do you hope to execute it? Write down your goals in as much specific detail as possible. When things aren't going well and you feel like giving up, return to this list of goals. Read them again, and refuse to take 'no' for an answer when pursuing your dream.

Business Knowledge
As previously noted, many good therapists lack good business

skills. The good news is that this is something that may be learned. Subscribe to business journals, read books on small business, or take a course at your local community college. You may also check to see if there is a Small Business Association in your area. This association consists of businessmen who volunteer their time and talents to help other businesses get off the ground. Also check with your local Chamber of Commerce and your local library for workshops on successful small businesses.

Organizational Skills
Look at your desk right now. Is it orderly, or chaotic? Think about your general organizational skills. If you are currently in practice at an agency, are your case notes up to date? How about your billing? How many things on your 'to do' list are checked off, and how many remain?
If you don't already possess at least some organizational skills, then you are going to have a hard time in private practice. It's okay if you lack a talent for this aspect of private practice. It's a skill that can be learned with practice. As a private practice clinician, the ultimate responsibility for your record-keeping is your own. If organizational skills are not a natural strength for you, you may want to work on this skill set before considering going into business for yourself.

Record Keeping Skills
Accurate and up-to-date records are the lifeblood of a successful business practice. This means not only keeping your case notes and clinical records up to date, but also your book keeping, accounting, and invoicing. If you accept insurance, you will also need to keep your insurance records current, and monitor which bills have been paid and which haven't.
If you are a single individual considering opening a private practice, the amount of paperwork for someone with little or no accounting and bookkeeping experience can be overwhelming. If this is the case, I would strongly advise seeking help from an accountant and/or an attorney. It doesn't take much to get behind on record keeping, and once you do, it can lead to errors, fines, and penalties come tax time.

Communication Skills
Therapists and counselors are trained to be good communicators; even so, the business world has its own lingo and jargon. It really

can be like learning a new language to dive into the world of private practice entrepreneurship. Your program probably taught you what a DSM-V is, but do you know what an EOB is? Or an EAP? Or an HMO? Your communication skills also come into play when seeking and making referrals, and when advertising. It is a violation of most ethical codes to misrepresent your skills and training, so you will be required to have excellent communication skills to be able to sell yourself without misrepresenting yourself.

A Sense of Adventure
If you're not comfortable taking risks, then private practice is not for you. The simple act of opening the doors to a private practice facility is itself a risky venture, especially in a market that is already saturated. It helps to think of what unique skills you will be bringing to the market that aren't already out there. What services can you offer, and how can you do it differently than everyone else?
A caveat here: Risk-taking and a sense of adventure do not extend to the realm of engaging in ethically questionable practices. Before taking any course of action, always examine your ethical code and consult with an attorney if necessary.

Confidence
If you don't believe in yourself, why should your clients believe in you? The bad news about starting a private practice is that if you believe you cannot do it, you're right. The good news about starting a private practice is that if you believe you *can* do it, you're right as well.
Try this: Ask yourself, on a scale of 1 to 10 with "1" being "not sure at all" and '10' being "100% certain," "How much do I feel that starting a private practice is the right career choice for me?"
Now, ask yourself, using the same scale, "How confident am I that I can build a successful private practice?"
The answer to the first question tells you how passionate you are about starting a private practice. The answer to the second question tells you how confident you are in your own ability to build a successful private practice. Out of all of the characteristics that are necessary for success in this business, passion and confidence are the most important. If your answer to either question above was lower than 5, you're not ready to start a private practice yet.
If you're not confident that you possess all the skills needed to run a private practice, you may always try a 'fake it 'til you make

it' approach. In your business dealings, act with confidence even though you might not feel confident on the inside. The more you practice this attitude of confidence, the more naturally confident you will become.

Pros and Cons of Private Practice

Is private practice right for you? Before making any decision, read over the material in this chapter again. Make notes on any pros and cons you might find in the topics above. Next, using the chart below as a template, write the pros and cons of starting a private practice in the appropriate quadrant. The decision being made is whether or not you're ready to start your own private practice. There are two columns in the chart. The first column is 'Start a Private Practice,' and the second is, "Don't Start a Private Practice.' On the left side of the chart are two rows, labeled 'Costs' and 'Benefits.' In the 'Costs' row, list all of the costs associated with starting a private practice in the first column, and all the costs of *not* starting a private practice in the second column. The costs don't have to be financial. They could also be costs on your time, costs to your family, costs to friends, costs due to emotional stress, etc.

Now do the same thing with the 'Benefits' row, starting with 'Benefits of starting a private practice,' then moving on to 'Benefits of not starting a private practice.' When you have finished filling out the chart, you'll be ready to make your decision. It may help to make a copy of this page and to make notes on the copy. Alternately you may just use a sheet of paper folded into quarters.

SHOULD I START A PRIVATE PRACTICE?

	Start a Private Practice	Don't Start a Private Practice
Costs		
Benefits		

Making Your Decision

After you have filled out the chart on the previous page, the next thing to do is to score each response. To do that, you would rate each response on a scale of 1 to 10, with 1 being 'not very important' to 10 being 'most important.'

The reason for scoring each item is that some items may be more important to you than others. For example, you might list a couple of items in the 'Benefits of private practice' column. Let's say those two items were, "Being my own boss," and "Getting to spend more time helping my patients." Let's further suppose that while being your own boss is nice, it's not as important to you as the opportunity to help your patients. So you might rate 'being my own boss' around a one or a two, while you might rate, 'getting to spend more time helping my patients' around a nine or a ten. The point here is that you might have a lot of items in one of the columns, but those things might not be as important as some of the items in another column.

When I graduated from my Masters program, I got a job offer in New York. At that time, I did a chart like this to decide whether to take the job. There were a lot of items in the 'plus' column for taking the job: Great pay, moving to New York, great agency, etc. but there was only one item in the 'Don't move to New York' column. It just so happened that at the time my daughter lived with her mother at the time, and if I moved to New York I'd only get to see her for a couple of weeks in the summer. So that one item in the 'Don't move to New York' column outweighed all the items in the 'Move to New York' column.

After you have scored each item, add up all the scores. The column with the highest score wins.

I wouldn't advise you to only do this exercise once, and then use that one-time result to make a decision. You should spend a bit of time gathering information first. As you learn more about what's involved in starting your own private practice, you'll have a better understanding of what it takes, and your answers on this chart may change. The best approach is to do this chart several times over a period of weeks or months as you gather information, keeping a running total of your results as you go. Be realistic and honest with yourself as you complete the chart each time. The average answer over a period of time will most likely be the correct one.

2 Types of Business Entity

So you've decided to start your own private practice. The next step is to determine the business structure of your organization. There are plenty of types to choose from. Each has its advantages and disadvantages. In this chapter we'll look at the various types and discuss these advantages and disadvantages.

In most states in the United States, if you decide on a business structure that would require incorporation of any sort, you would file with the Secretary of State for the state in which the business will be incorporated. There is a list of contact information for the Secretaries of State for each state in the U.S. in Appendix C at the end of this book. In the states of Alaska, Hawaii, and Utah, there is no Secretary of State. In those states many duties of a Secretary of State fall within the domain of the Lieutenant Governor.

Some forms of business structure do not require registration with the Secretary of State, since they are not corporations. Laws vary from state to state, so if in doubt, consult your Secretary of State or your attorney. It is advisable to avoid any business venture without first consulting with an attorney or an accountant who is competent in the area of business law.

Look over the information below, and determine which structure appears to meet your business needs. Once you've made a preliminary decision, investigate everything you can about your chosen business structure and how to implement it in your state. Consult with your attorney and your local Secretary of State to see if the advantages of your chosen structure are right for you, and to make sure that the advantages of your chosen structure outweigh the disadvantages. If the information looks good, move forward with creating your business entity.

The types of entity we will be discussing in this chapter are: Sole Proprietorship, Partnership, Limited Partnership, Limited Liability Corporation (LLC), Corporation, and Non-Profit Corporation. If your state offers types of business entity not discussed in this chapter, you may wish to investigate further with your local Small Business Association or Chamber of Commerce.

Sole Proprietorship

In a sole proprietorship, you own the business entirely to yourself, and are responsible for everything to do with it. The advantage to a sole proprietorship is that it is cheap and easy to start. In most cases all you would need is a Certificate of Authority stating that you are the person authorized to speak for your business. In some states this isn't even a requirement. The only cost for setting up a sole proprietorship is just a business license, if your local area requires one. If you are in a rural setting or outside of the city limits, you may not even need a business license. Check with your local Tax Assessor's office to find out for sure.

Another advantage of the sole proprietorship is that all of the profit from the business is yours. You are your own boss, and you reap all the rewards of the business. You also do all the work, and have the final say on any business decisions.

Disadvantages of a sole proprietorship include the fact that you have no limited liability in this type of business entity. This means that if you are sued, or if your business otherwise fails, creditors can come after your personal assets as well as your business assets. All the financial risk is yours and yours alone.

Another disadvantage is that if you're sick, or if you take a vacation, or if any other emergency comes up requiring your absence, you don't make any money for the period of time that you are gone. While it's nice to be able to take a day or a week off any time you want, you also have to consider the fact that time off equals time with no income.

Since you do all the work in a sole proprietorship, you have to honestly ask yourself if you have all the skills required to run a successful private practice. As a private practice clinician in a sole proprietorship, you will have to wear many hats. In addition to having exceptional clinical skills, you will have to be an expert in accounting, marketing, bookkeeping, branding, public speaking, networking, medical billing, and resource management. If you lack skills in some of these areas, you might be able to hire experts. If you lack accounting skills, you can hire an accountant. But if you lack public speaking skills and are asked to present a workshop on services offered by your business, it's hard to hire someone to speak for you.

If you do a realistic inventory of your skills and talents, and decide that you still have what it takes, and don't mind putting your personal assets at risk should the business fail, then this might be the type of business entity for you.

'Doing Business As' (DBA)

A 'Doing Business As,' or 'DBA,' is a sole proprietorship or a general partnership that is doing business under a name other than the name of the owner(s). It is not a separate legal business entity from its owner, but it is simply using a different name. The owner of such a business is still liable for all of the debt incurred under the DBA name, and receives all profits of the business under the DBA name. All income from the DBA is added to the owner's individual tax return, and is not filed separately under the business's name.

A DBA name can be chosen for several reasons. One of these reasons is that the owner does not wish to use his name for the name of the business. For example, I used Mindfulness-Based Family Therapy as my DBA rather than doing business under my own name, Charlton Hall. If I just used my given name, there is no way that people would know what sort of business it might be. But by using Mindfulness-Based Family Therapy, my potential clients automatically know that it is a therapy business, and that my primary therapeutic orientation is mindfulness-based, and that I provide services to families as well as to individuals.

Another reason for using a DBA is if I have multiple businesses under the same umbrella. Suppose I own a chain of clinics throughout the Southeast. In order to distinguish them from one another, I would give them all different names, under the same business entity. One might be Charlton Hall Counseling, DBA Greenville Therapy Group. Another might be Charlton Hall Counseling, DBA Spartanburg Therapy Group. In this case, both Greenville Therapy Group and Spartanburg Therapy Group would be owned by the same company, Charlton Hall Counseling, but each would have a distinct 'doing business as' name.

The main purpose of a DBA name is for banking. Suppose I don't have a DBA banking account. If that's the case, I'd only be able to accept checks made out to me personally. But if I have a DBA banking account such as

Charlton Hall, MMFT, LMFT, DBA Mindfulness-Based Family Therapy, then my patients may make their checks out to Mindfulness-Based Family Therapy, and the bank will allow me to deposit them under that name. Although LLCs have replaced DBAs in many states due to the relative ease of filing requirements for LLCs, people still use DBAs on occasion. Consult with your bank or your attorney to find out if there are any advantages to using a DBA for your private practice.

Partnership

This type of business structure consists of you and one or more partners. It is similar to a sole proprietorship, except that you're including more people under the umbrella of the entity.

One of the advantages of a partnership is that, like a sole proprietorship, it is cheap and easy to start. Unlike a sole proprietorship, there is the extra expense of having a legal contract drawn up between the partners, specifying the legal responsibilities of each partner.

Another advantage of a partnership is that all the profit belongs to you and your partner alone. There are no shareholders to pay. You and your partner are your own bosses, and you share all the rewards, and all the risks, of the business together. But like a sole proprietorship, if you have a partnership, both you and your partner will be expected to wear a lot of hats. Do you both have the skills necessary to make a go of it? Ideally, in a partnership your strengths and weaknesses should complement each other. Perhaps you're not good at accounting, but your partner is. Or maybe you're good at marketing, and your partner is not. In an ideal situation, you should select your partner based on what he or she is bringing to the table in terms of resources, and not just because you're friends with a mutual interest. Partnerships force you to learn the difference between friendship and business.

It's been said that whatever direction your friendship is going, if you go into business with a friend it'll help you get there more quickly. If you're great friends with your business partner and can stand stress and tribulation together with no ill effects, then going into a partnership is likely to make your friendship stronger. If, on the other hand, you have a shaky friendship, the trials and tribulations of a business partnership are likely to help it go downhill that much more rapidly. I'd do some serious soul-searching before dragging friendship into the business world.

One of the disadvantages of a partnership is that you and your partner have no limited liability. Both you and your partner are responsible for all debts incurred by the business, and for all financial liability of your organization. This means that if your company goes into debt, the debt isn't split 50/50 between you and your partner. Both of you are liable for *all* of the debt.

Another disadvantage is that if you haven't spelled out in detail which partner is responsible for which part of the workload, you're headed for potential trouble. Will you both be responsible for booking your own appointments? Will you buy your own office supplies, or will you share? If you're splitting utilities, but your partner likes to leave the lights on all the time, how will you address that? These are all issues to consider before going into a partnership.

Limited Partnership

The difference between a partnership and a limited partnership is that in a limited partnership there are 'limited partners' who are silent partners. A silent partner is a partner who may contribute financial resources to the business, but who does not get involved in the day-to-day operations of the business. Such partners look upon the business as an investment opportunity. The silent partners invest funds and resources, and the general partners run the business.

In most states a limited partnership is a legal business entity, and you will probably have to file such a partnership with your Secretary of State. There are some tax benefits for this type of business entity in most cases, but check with your attorney or accountant to make sure that these benefits are available in your state. Another advantage of a limited partnership is that it does offer some protection from liability in case of a financial disaster. This type of business arrangement is attractive to investors who believe in a company or its product, but who do not want to be involved in the day-to-day operations. For this type of business arrangement, you will need an attorney to draw up a contract specifically stating the responsibilities of each partner. This is true for both the general partners and the silent partners.

One disadvantage to a limited partnership is that there is a greater risk and liability on the general partners than on the silent partners. Since the general partners run the business, they bear a greater responsibility for the business decisions they make. This can be an advantage if you're one of the silent partners, since silent partners don't actually get involved in running the business.

Limited partnerships must hold at least one meeting per year to inform the silent partners of the status of the business. Reports of these meetings must be filed and archived, and made available upon request. Usually records of these meetings must be retained indefinitely. Check with your attorney for details on how these reports must be filed.

Limited Liability Company (LLC)

A Limited Liability Company, or LLC, is a midway step between a sole proprietorship or partnership and a full corporation. In general an LLC offers more protection from liability than a sole proprietorship or partnership, but less liability protection than a corporation.

In most states you have tax flexibility with an LLC. What this means is that you can choose to pay taxes on the business yourself, or you can create a fictitious entity, similar to a corporation, that pays taxes for the business. It's also easier to set up an LLC than it is to set up a corporation. In most cases, you just fill out a form that you'd obtain from your Secretary of State, and send it in with the appropriate supplemental forms (tax information, business licenses, etc.) and the filing fee. This is a little more difficult than setting up a sole proprietorship or partnership, but a lot less difficult than setting up a corporation.

There is also less paperwork with an LLC than there would be with a corporation. In most states you simply create a Limited Liability Company Operating Agreement in which you spell out the details of how your business will operate. This is similar to the bylaws filed by corporations, but without the need for approval by a Board of Directors. If you choose not to file an LLC Operating Agreement, most states will allow you to be governed by the default LLC operating rules and regulations established by the state.

The 'limited liability' of a Limited Liability Company means that you are able to shield your personal assets from seizure or forfeiture to some extent should your business venture fail. For the most part, an LLC allows you to keep your business and personal assets separate.

Another advantage of an LLC is that you can offer shares to investors, and therefore raise capital to run your business. LLCs 'sell shares' by selling a percentage interest in the equity of the company. In doing so, the seller is purchasing the right to participate in the management of the company. Restrictions on how these shares may be offered vary from state to state, so be sure you understand how these laws and regulations operate in your state before choosing this type of business entity structure. As always, consult with your attorney to make sure you understand the legal requirements.

A disadvantage of an LLC is that the tax flexibility can sometimes backfire on you. Self-employment taxes can be higher than taxes on corporations, so if you set up your LLC in such a way that you have to pay self-employment tax, it could wind up costing you more at tax time. Since these tax laws vary widely from state to state, you should consult with an attorney before making a final decision.

Another disadvantage to an LLC is that you can only sell shares privately, and not on a public exchange. While it is possible to convert an LLC to a corporation should you decide to expand and 'go public' with your stock offerings, it is usually easier to create a corporation from scratch than it is to backtrack and convert an LLC to a corporation.

A final disadvantage to LLCs is that they require more paperwork, regulation and report writing than a sole proprietorship or a partnership. So if you're a lone clinician planning to start a private practice on your own without partners, bear in mind that LLC filing requirements will be just one more thing you'll have to add to your plate as you do your monthly paperwork.

Of all the forms of business structure selected by private practice clinicians, the LLC is the most popular. Although it has more filing and paperwork requirements than a sole proprietorship or a partnership, the added limited liability makes this very attractive to first-time business owners of all kinds. This is especially true for therapists and counselors starting out in private practice.

Corporations

A corporation is a fictitious entity with a Board of Directors. It is 'fictitious' because it is viewed as an artificial person. The word 'corporation' comes from the Latin for 'body,' and a corporation is a legally-defined body that is created solely for the purpose of doing business. There are C-Corporations and S-Corporations. A C-Corporation pays taxes through the entity of the corporation, and an S-Corporation is taxed like a partnership or a sole proprietorship. Many startup corporations, especially the small ones, set up as S-Corporations in order to avoid double taxation. In a C-Corporation income and losses are taxed at the corporate level, and then again when they are given back to corporate shareholders in the form of profits. In general, S-Corporations avoid this by taxing income as personal rather than corporate gain. There are tax advantages to either form of corporation, depending on the needs of the business. An in-depth discussion of corporate tax law could fill another book, and is outside the scope of this book. If you are considering opening a corporation, consult with an attorney with expertise in corporate law in order to determine the tax advantages and disadvantages for what you have in mind.

A major advantage to corporations is that all assets and liabilities of the business are held by the business. In case of default, creditors cannot come after the personal assets of the owners of the corporation. All financial liability is held by the corporation itself.

Corporations are also easier to finance because you are allowed to sell stock in the corporation. If you have a good business plan and a good business concept, investors will seek you out to invest in your business. Banks are usually also more willing to work with corporations than with individuals because the overall structure of a corporation is more stable. Corporations quite often outlive their founders. The longest lived corporation in history, the Japanese construction company Kongo Gumi, lasted 1,428 years before it closed its doors. If banks loan money to individual sole proprietors, and those proprietors pass away, they may not be able to collect their debt. But corporations can be around for centuries, and banks will always be able to demand payment from them for as long as they exist, therefore banks are generally more willing to loan money to corporations.

Corporations can also be publicly traded. This means they can be listed on various stock exchanges. This publicity gives corporations greater public recognition and tends to lend legitimacy to business ventures; at least in the public's eye. If you've taken the time and trouble to incorporate your business, people tend to think that you're serious about succeeding.

Along with the increased protection from liability that corporations afford, there is also increased responsibility. Corporations must publish annual business reports, and usually quarterly reports as well. As a publicly-traded corporation, government entities have the right to access your books for purposes of audit at any time. There are also quite a number of legal procedures that corporations have to follow in all of their business dealings. These procedures vary widely from state to state.

Since the Board of Directors runs a corporation, it is possible for the original owner(s) of the corporation to lose control of the business. If the Board decides to vote you out, you're out.

Regardless of the additional legal obligations and filing requirements, the benefits of a corporation are often attractive to mid-to-large sized startups. If this form of business entity appeals to you, consult with your attorney to discuss in depth how your local and state laws would benefit your private practice in a corporate structure.

Non-Profit Corporation

A non-profit corporation is a corporation founded for a charitable, educational, or religious purpose. This is a popular form of business organization for organizations that offer mental health services. One reason for this is that there are federal, state, and local grants that are available for such organizations. Another reason is that such clinics can provide mental health services at a reduced rate for underserved populations due to the fact that non-profits rely on grants and donations for funding rather than on insurance companies and out-of-pocket clients.

There are two general types of non-profit: Board-directed and member-directed. A board-directed non-profit has a Board of Directors who make policy decisions and keep the organization running. In most states, members of the board are not allowed to receive a salary or other compensation for their services. These positions must be filled by volunteers. A member-directed non-profit has members, and this body of members votes on policies and procedures for the organization. Members may not receive compensation for their services.

Many states also allow for a hybrid of these two, in which there is a

Board of Directors that oversees day-to-day operations, and a body of members who vote on major decisions.

Non-profits are usually tax exempt. This means that if you apply for, and receive, a non-profit designation from the Internal Revenue Service, most of your assets are granted tax exemption. This tax exempt status usually makes you eligible to receive grants, donations and gifts on a tax-free basis. Donors may then deduct their gifts to your organization on their own income taxes. In order to become a tax-exempt organization you must apply to the Internal Revenue Service using Form 1023. This cannot be done until your Articles of Incorporation have been approved and registered by your state's Secretary of State.

For most non-profits related to mental and behavioral health, the appropriate designation would be 501(c)(3). According to the Internal Revenue Service's website, a 501(c)(3) non-profit would fall into the following categories:

- 501(c)(3): Religious, Educational, Charitable, Scientific, Literary, Testing for Public Safety, to Foster National or International Amateur Sports Competition, or Prevention of Cruelty to Children or Animals Organizations.
- Other possible types of non-profit that a private practice mental health clinician might consider would be the following:
- 501(c)(4): Civic Leagues, Social Welfare Organizations, and Local Associations of Employees

If you are considering a non-profit, and are not sure which type would suit your proposed organization, consult with an attorney specializing in non-profit law. You may also check to see if your state has a statewide association of non-profit organizations. Such an association can be a valuable resource for information on starting your own non-profit.

In addition to tax exempt status and being able to receive grants, donations and gifts as charitable donations, no-profits protect members of the organization from personal financial liability, just as other types of corporations do. A non-profit may also insure continuity after the death or retirement of its founders.

If your non-profit has employees, they may also be eligible for employee benefits from various government and private entities that offer special incentives for non-profit employees.

A drawback to running a non-profit is the large amount of paperwork involved. In addition to filing periodic revenue reports with the Internal Revenue Service and your state and local tax authorities, any grants that you receive will also have mandatory reporting guidelines. If a government or private donor is giving you money to run your programs, they're going to want to see that their investment is yielding results. Most grants come with mandatory evaluation instruments and reporting requirements for this purpose.

Ironically, a non-profit can be one of the most expensive types of business entity to start up. You have to hire an attorney whose expertise is in non-profit corporate law. You'll have to select a Board of Directors and an Executive Director, and these individuals will have to come together to draft bylaws for the organization, preferably under the direction of an attorney knowledgeable about bylaws. The key to bylaw writing is to make the bylaws specific enough to give your non-profit a structure, but flexible enough to allow for change over time as your non-profit evolves.

If you got into a healing profession because you wanted to make a difference, and you don't mind the extra paperwork, filing requirements, and legal restrictions on a non-profit, this may be the type of organization for your private practice. Grants and funding allow such organizations to serve those who might not otherwise be able to afford your services.

A Note on Business Names

Your Secretary of State will not allow you to incorporate any business entity that has a name identical to an organization that is already in existence. The Secretary of State also does not mediate disputes over corporate names. If you have a name that you wish to reserve for your corporation, you should contact the Trademarks Division of your state, and not the Secretary of State.

Some states will allow you to reserve a corporation name until the lengthy process of incorporating is complete. Check with your Secretary of State's office to see if this is a service they offer. Registration of a new corporation requires preparation of many legal documents which must be registered and filed. This must be done before the Internal Revenue Service will recognize your organization, and most state and local governments require federal recognition before they will recognize your organization. This process can sometimes take up to a year to complete. It may even take longer if there are any problems with any of the paperwork or filings along the way. If you don't want someone else to grab up the name of your organization before you have an opportunity to complete the process, you should reserve your corporate name as soon as possible.

3 Taxes and Licenses

Since tax laws vary from state to state, a comprehensive overview is beyond the scope of this book. For specific details on local tax law in your area, consult with your attorney or accountant. There are, however, some general criteria that would apply in all cases. In this chapter we'll discuss some of these criteria.

After you have decided on the form and structure of your business entity, you will need to open a bank account. Most solo private practice clinicians open either a Limited Liability Company or a Sole Proprietorship, so we'll assume that you'll be using one of these forms of business structure. If you are using a different form, you will need to consult with your accountant and your bank to determine your particular needs.

The first thing you will need to do after creating your business entity is to open a bank account in the name of the business. When you open your bank account for your private practice, you will be asked to supply a tax identification number. If you have a sole proprietorship, you may elect to use your Social Security number if you wish. I wouldn't recommend it for the reasons cited below, but if you do wish to use your Social Security number as your business's tax identification number, there is nothing legally stopping you, as long as your business does not have employees, and you never plan to have employees in the future. If you ever plan to have any employees, you will need an Employer Identification Number (EIN) from the Internal Revenue Service. Additionally, if you plan to operate as any form of corporation or as a partnership, you will need to have an EIN. The Internal Revenue Service lists the requirements for an EIN on their website at www.irs.gov.

The first reason not to use your Social Security number is that if you don't have a separate tax identification number for your business, it will be difficult to distinguish personal transactions from business transactions at tax time. Another is that if you plan to take insurance, the insurance companies will request your tax identification number on all their paperwork, and if you use your Social Security number, it will be circulating throughout all the insurance companies you work with. This means that anyone who works with any insurance company will have access to your personal Social Security number.

Finally, insurance companies print your private practice's information on their Explanation of Benefits (EOB) forms that they send to their clients. So this means that if you use your personal Social Security number, then any of your patients who use insurance will eventually have access to your personal information. This is definitely not a good idea, because with your Social Security number, your patients will be able to find out everything else about you, including your home telephone number, where you live, names of your spouse, children, and other family members, and previous employment history.

If you plan to have any employees at any time in the future, you will need a separate tax identification number anyway, so you might as well go ahead and get one at the start, and save yourself the headache of trying to transfer from one tax identification number to another as your business grows. If you try to change tax identification numbers once a business has been established, you will have to change the number with all insurance companies you do business with. You'll also have to change it with any other vendors, with your bank, and with all of your creditors. In some cases you may have to close out your bank account and open another one with the new tax identification number. So it's definitely better and less time-consuming to go ahead and get a separate tax identification number at the start.

The Federal Employer Identification Number, or FEIN, is also known as an Employer Identification Number (EIN), or a Tax Identification Number (TIN). These are all labels for the same thing. In general, it is referred to as 'EIN' when used in tax matters related to employees, and as 'TIN' when referring to general matters related to federal and state taxes. The major difference between an EIN and a TIN is that an EIN is assigned by the Internal Revenue Service to be used as the tax identification number for a specific business, while a TIN refer to either an EIN or a personal Social Security number.

Although the EIN or FEIN is called the *'Employer* Identification Number' or 'Federal *Employer* Identification Number,' you may still need such a number even if you don't have employees and have no plans for having employees in the future. Although an EIN is not mandatory for sole proprietorships and some types of partnerships, it is mandatory for any other type of business structure, including Limited Liability Companies (LLCs), C-Corporations, S-Corporations, Limited Partnerships, and Non-profit Corporations. This keeps business transactions separate from personal transactions, and lets the Internal Revenue Service know which transactions are associated with your private practice.

Applying for a Federal Employer Identification Number is relatively painless and can be completed online. The entire process takes no more than thirty minutes at most. To download an application for FEIN, visit http://www.irs.gov/pub/irs-pdf/fss4.pdf.

Licenses

If you are a Marriage and Family Therapist, this book assumes that you already have a license to practice Marriage and Family Therapy in the United States. Marriage and Family Therapy (MFT) licensure is regulated at the state level. In some states, MFT Interns or associates are allowed to practice as long as they are under supervision by a licensed Marriage and Family Therapy Supervisor. If you are an intern or associate, check with your local licensure board and/or your supervisor before going into private practice. If you are a fully licensed Marriage and Family Therapist or other mental health professional, then you are ready to open your own private practice.

Once you have decided on a structure for your private practice, you will need to determine which types of business licensure may be required in your area in order to open for business. If your office will be within the city limits, you will probably need a business license. Check with your local tax assessor to see what sort of license might be required. If you have a local Chamber of Commerce, they can tell you what sort of licenses might be required for your business as well. Many Chambers of Commerce offer business startup kits with such information.

If your private practice office will be in a rural area, it is possible that you might not need a business license, since business licenses are usually issued by towns or cities. If you are outside of the city limits, check with your county's tax assessor to see if they require a county business license. If not, you may not need a business license.

You may also be required to obtain an Occupancy Permit. These are generally issued by the local Building Inspector's office, although they may sometimes be issued by a different office. An Occupancy Permit requires a site inspection to make sure there are no safety concerns with the building before allowing it to open for business. Once the inspector has checked your premises, he may require some modifications before granting a permit. Common suggestions include fire door access, fire extinguishers, smoke alarms and safety routes. Once your building has been declared safe for occupancy, the Occupancy Permit will be granted.

Some state and local ordinances require handicapped accessibility for any buildings being used for healthcare purposes. This includes mental health. So when you are selecting your office space, ask if it is handicapped accessible. If you plan to take insurance, EAPs or HMOs, be aware that they tend to give preferential treatment and referrals to private practitioners whose buildings are handicapped accessible. Some will not work with clinicians unless their buildings are accessible to all. It's far easier and less expensive to find an office that meets federal and state regulations for handicap accessibility than it is to try to retrofit an existing space. So add this to your list of considerations as you search for office space. Additionally, some building inspectors will require your building to be handicapped accessible before they will grant an Occupancy Permit. Check your local regulations to see if this is a requirement on any building you're considering.

Another license you may consider obtaining is a retail license. Retail licenses are granted at the state level, usually by your state's Department of Revenue. If you are only engaging in therapy, you will not need a retail license, but if you plan to sell anything taxable in your private practice, you will need to get one. Why would a therapist need a retail license? If you plan to sell books, audio recordings, DVDs, or other merchandise as a supplement to your therapy practice, you will probably have to charge sales tax on these items. Books and supplemental materials can be both a steady source of additional income and a great way to supplement your therapy practice with 'homework' assignments, so this line of marketing is well worth considering. If you choose to go this route, you will need a retail license.

When you go to open your business bank account, most banks will ask for a copy of your business license, if you are required to have one, and your tax identification number. So you will need to obtain these before you apply for a business bank account. Most insurance companies, EAPs and HMOs will also ask you for your tax identification number, as they are required to report any revenue paid to you, and your TIN is necessary in order to report your income to the IRS.

Liability Issues

If you are in a sole proprietorship that intends to use a 'Doing Business As' (DBA) account, be aware that such an account does not offer any protection from liability for financial losses. Your personal assets can be seized to pay for any debts incurred by the business. As a sole proprietor, you are still responsible for all of your business dealings, and for any debts incurred by your business. This means that if someone decided to sue your business, they would be suing you personally, and you would be responsible for any liabilities incurred under such a lawsuit.

This liability also applies to tax debts. If you are indebted to state or federal agencies for back taxes, and you only have a sole proprietorship under a DBA bank account, you are personally liable for any unpaid tax debts. In some cases, state or federal tax agents may be able to seize your assets for failure to pay those debts.

Estimated Taxes

If you are self-employed in a private practice, your income is not subject to tax withholding. Because of this fact, you will have to pay *estimated tax*. You will use estimated tax to pay your income taxes and your self-employment taxes. If you are self-employed, estimated tax is a requirement. If you don't pay enough withholding on your estimated tax payments, or if you don't pay them by the due date, you may be charged a penalty at tax time. This penalty may be due even if you are supposed to get a refund on your taxes.

If you are filing your federal income tax as a sole proprietor, a partner, an S-Corporation shareholder, or a self-employed individual, you will have to pay estimated taxes. If your private practice is set up under some other business entity, then the business will pay your withholding when it issues you a paycheck. For 2013 the form used to pay estimated tax is Form 1040-ES, the *Estimated Tax for Individuals* form that may be downloaded at http://www.irs.gov/pub/irs-pdf/f1040es.pdf. Instructions for filling out this form are included on IRS Publication 505, *Tax Withholding and Estimated Tax*. You may download this publication at http://www.irs.gov/pub/irs-pdf/p505.pdf.

If your private practice is a corporation, you would use IRS Form 1120-W, *Estimated Tax for Corporation*. You may download this form at http://www.irs.gov/pub/irs-pdf/f1120w.pdf. Instructions for filling out this form are contained in IRS Publication 542, *Corporations*. This publication may be downloaded by visiting http://www.irs.gov/pub/irs-pdf/p542.pdf.

In general you must pay estimated taxes if you are a sole proprietor, S-Corporation shareholder, partner, or self-employed individual who expects to owe $1,000 or more when you file your annual tax return. If you are filing as a corporation, you usually have to make estimated tax payments if you expect to owe taxes of $500 or more for the year.

If your private practice is set up in such a way that you receive a periodic paycheck instead of a share of the profits from the business, then your accountant can set up this paycheck in such a way that your taxes and other withholdings are deducted from your paycheck, thus saving you from having to make estimated tax payments. In such a case, you would file a Form W-4 with the Internal Revenue Service and your accountant would send the taxes and withholdings.

According to the Internal Revenue Service's website, you do not have to pay estimated taxes if you meet *all* of the following conditions:
- You had no tax liability for the prior year
- You were a U.S. citizen or resident for the whole year
- Your prior tax year covered a 12 month period
- You had no tax liability for the prior year if your total tax was zero or you did not have to file an income tax return

If you have little or no experience with tax law, you will definitely want to have your accountant or bookkeeper help out with paying your estimated taxes. In order to figure out how much to withhold for each estimated tax period, you will first need to calculate your expected adjusted gross income, your taxable income, amount of taxes you owe on this income, any deductions you might be eligible for, and any tax credits you might have for the year. When doing this it helps to look at the previous year's tax returns in order to be able to make an educated guess as to what these numbers might be. The difficulty here, of course, is that if you are just starting your private practice you will have no numbers from the previous year, and will have to rely on an educated guess as to what these numbers might be. This is why it is critical to engage the services of an accountant. This is especially true if you have no previous experience with taxes yourself. If your educated guesses turn out to be wrong, it could really cost you at tax time. A good accountant will have a reasonable estimate of what your tax liability will be, based on similar businesses in your area. If your accountant has no experience with therapy offices, you may want to consider finding one who does.

Estimate taxes are paid quarterly. This means that there are four opportunities during a given tax year to adjust your estimated taxes in order to avoid penalties. For example, if your estimated income for the first quarter is higher than expected, you can adjust the amount you pay in the second quarter to reflect this change. If your estimated income for the first quarter is lower than expected, you have the option of adjusting your holdings downward so that you get to keep more of that quarterly income, or to leave your withholdings the same in order to cover any unforeseen tax liabilities at the end of the year. If you overpay on your quarterly estimates, you can always get it back at the end of the year in the form of a tax refund, but if you underpay, you will have to scramble at the end of the year to find the funds to pay.

You are required to pay estimated taxes four times per year, on a quarterly basis. Each quarter has a specific due date. If you haven't paid your quarterly estimated taxes on time, you may be charged a penalty at the end of the year when you file your tax return.

You may pay your quarterly estimated taxes using the Electronic Federal Tax Payment System (EFTPS). This is probably the easiest way to do so, as it does not rely on sending hard copies of all of your tax data. The EFTPS may be accessed online at https://www.eftps.gov. You may also enroll to use the EFTPS at that link. When enrolling you will need your Federal Employer Identification Number (FEIN) or other tax identification number (TIN), so have that information handy before logging in.

If you don't pay enough taxes on your estimated tax payments, you may have to pay a penalty for underpayment at the end of the tax year. In general you will be able to avoid this penalty if you owe less than $1,000 in taxes after credits and other withholdings, or if you have paid at least 90% of the taxes due for the current year during your quarterly estimated tax payments, or if you paid 100% of the taxes owe on the prior year's return, assuming you were in private practice for the duration of the previous year.

You may also avoid a penalty if your failure to make payments was caused by injury, illness, natural disaster, or other unusual circumstances that made it difficult or impossible to pay your taxes. In any such case the failure to make payment would have to be due to a reasonable economic hardship and not due to a willful neglect to pay. A note of caution here: The Internal Revenue Service gets to decide what constitutes a 'reasonable economic hardship;' you don't. So before neglecting to pay estimated taxes, consult with a good tax attorney.

The best way to avoid penalties and unpleasant surprises is to set up a good accounting system at the beginning, and to follow it diligently. Let's face it, accounting is boring, but necessary. It's been estimated that 15%-20% of startup businesses in the United States fail solely from poor accounting practices. You don't want to be one of those startup businesses, so always budget your time wisely to include time to do a proper job of accounting.

Necessity of Good Accounting Practices

As noted in the previous section, accounting is boring. If you're like most therapists, you didn't choose your profession so you could sit behind a desk crunching numbers all day. Yet accounting is a necessary evil if you intend to stay in business. Even a small accounting error can make or break a therapy business. If you are not comfortable with keeping up with your accounting on a regular basis, then by all means secure the service of a good accountant or bookkeeper. It's better to have the out-of-pocket expense of a bookkeeper than it is to lose your business due to an accounting mistake.

The first step in assuring that your accounting stays current is to establish a schedule. Some tasks will need to be done on a quarterly basis, some on a monthly basis, some on a weekly basis, and some on a daily basis. For example, tax-related accounting will need to be done on a quarterly basis. This means keeping all your estimated tax payments up-to-date and as accurate as possible. Your insurance billing will probably be done on a monthly basis. This means monthly billing to your insurance companies, and reconciling all billing statements with payments received. If you bill clients for your services rather than accepting payment when services are rendered, you will probably also be billing your clients on a monthly basis. It is best practices to enter all of your day-to-day accounting, such as daily payments received, daily expenses paid, and other daily income and expenses on a daily basis. This means that after a long day of seeing clients, you need to set aside at least an hour or two to reconcile the books before going home. If you can't find the time to do this on a daily basis, then it should, at minimum, be done on a weekly basis. Don't neglect this, as it can pile up fast!

A good part of a well-constructed accounting practice is a good business plan. If you've never written a business plan before, it's a good idea to read a few books on writing an effective one. You may also consult with other businesses or professionals with experience in writing business plans. If you have a college or university in your area, their business department can probably offer suggestions in this area.

A major part of any good business plan is financial planning. Where do you want your private practice to be in a year? In five years? What's your plan for getting there? How much will you spend on advertising and marketing? How much will you spend on expansion of the business? What are your businesses financial strengths? What are its financial weaknesses? What are the opportunities in your area? That is to say, what unique niches will your private practice fill that are not being addressed by other businesses in your region? A portion of your monthly budget should be set aside to address all of these issues.

Your business plan should also include a profit and loss projection for at least three years. If you are just starting up your practice, you will have to make educated guesses on these numbers, and then adjust accordingly as revenue comes in. You will want to track your revenue stream on an annual basis, as therapy tends to be a seasonal business. If you work with families, do you notice a dip in referrals for children when summer starts? If so, you will need to plan ahead for this dip in income. If you work in the addiction field, do you notice a peak in referrals during the holiday season as people get arrested for driving under the influence at various holiday roadblocks? If so, you will need to plan on how you may distribute any of these windfalls so that they can assist you financially during the less lucrative seasons.

Once you have plotted your projections for at least three years, you have a better understanding of where your business is going. This information can then be used to plan your strategies and objectives when planning your business's budget. This information will all have to be taken into consideration when drafting your accounting system.

Some other factors you may want to consider when setting up your accounting system:

Cash flow: You will need to account for your projected cash flow on an annual basis so that you will know when the lean times are coming. This will help you to be better prepared for times of lower cash flow.

Financial reporting: You will need a good financial software system to keep track of your cash flow. Requirements for such software vary widely based on the needs of your particular private practice. If you lack experience in this area, you may want to consult with an accountant. Some of this software can be quite expensive, and you don't want to waste money buying features you don't need. Any software package you purchase should, at a minimum, be able to generate profit and loss statements, balance sheets, performance-to-budget projections, cash flow reports, and analysis of accounts receivable and accounts payable.

Record keeping: If you are taking insurance payments, they have the right to audit your books at any time. If you are a licensed business, state, federal and local tax agents have the right to audit your books at any time. It is therefore essential that you keep your records up-to-date. You don't want to be working all night the night before an audit, trying to get your books current. The best practice in this case is to avoid letting them get behind in the first place. This means that you should keep all relevant documentation for your business. This includes bank statements, receipts, invoices, profit and loss statements, tax returns, tax receipts, balance sheets, accounting records, and any other documentation in which money came into or went out of the business.

Budgeting: A well-planned and executed budget is a necessity for any business. A good budget takes into account all money going out of a business and all money going into a business. An excellent budget plans for unforeseen financial emergencies and sets funds aside to address such crises. Two of the most common mistakes in drafting budgets are making them overly complicated and underestimating expenditures. Just to give you an example, when I first went into private practice I grossly underestimated the cost of office supplies. My intake packet is over 30 pages long, so for every new client I generate 30 printed pages. This includes the cost of the paper, the ink, and the file folder. This may seem negligible at first, but when you multiply it by the number of clients being seen on a monthly basis, it can add up. I'd budgeted for about $25-$30 per month for office supplies. The actual figure is closer to $100-$150. The best way to get accurate estimates for expenditures is to ask people already in the business. Pay special attention when they tell you what their unexpected expenditures were. When planning your budget, project it for at least twelve months. As your monthly profits and expenses come in, adjust your budget estimates accordingly. Some costs will be fixed, like office rent, professional organization dues, and license fees. Others may vary, like utility bills, office supplies, and advertising. Try to account for as many variables as possible when budgeting. The more accurate your budget is, the more your business will profit.

Good accounting should be planned for and scheduled during your daily and weekly activities. It shouldn't be looked on as something to do when you find some spare time. As the saying goes, "Time is money." This is especially true in the therapy business, as you are literally selling your time. This means that time spent accounting is an expense that should be budgeted during your weekly schedule. When planning your week, estimate how much time you will need to spend on accounting, and stick to it. Avoid the temptation to fill your accounting time with one more client. If you make bookkeeping and accounting part of your regular weekly schedule, you will never find yourself in a mad rush at tax time or prior to an audit. Never give in to the temptation to leave it until later. 'Later' may be too late!

4 Insurance Panels

In order to thrive in a private practice, you will need to rely on insurance panels and other third party payers. This is especially true if you are just starting out in private practice. Working with insurance companies can be frustrating, confusing and intimidating, but unfortunately they are a necessary evil for anyone who wants to make a living in private practice.

Before getting into the intricacies of working with insurance panels, let's talk about the alternatives. There are two possibilities for running a private practice without using insurance companies, EAPs and HMOs. One of these is to only work with people who can afford to pay for your services out-of-pocket, and the other is to offer a sliding fee scale based on income.

While it is (barely) possible to run a private practice without using insurance companies, it is pretty much impossible to start up a new Marriage and Family Therapy practice without relying on insurance. The only people I know who run out-of-pocket, fee-for-service practices are those who started out accepting insurance, then gradually weeded out insurance companies as their private practices and their own reputations as therapists and counselors grew. Unless you're a marketing genius or a well-established private practice clinician, you're most likely going to need to rely on third party payers to get you started.

The second alternative to an insurance-based practice is to offer a sliding fee scale. There are several problems with offering a sliding fee scale if you plan to make a go of it in private practice. One of these problems is that a sliding fee scale tends to devalue the services you provide as a therapist.

Suppose you wanted to take your partner out to dinner at a fancy restaurant. You pick up the menu and see that the entrees are $50 each. You call the waiter over and explain to him, "I can't afford to pay $50 for this entrée. Do you offer a sliding fee scale based on income?"

What do you suppose his answer would be?

Offering a sliding fee scale diminishes the value of your services. You've worked long and hard to get to this point, and you are entitled to be compensated for your hard work, just as any other professional would be entitled to be compensated for their hard work. By offering a sliding fee scale, you're telling your clients that your services aren't as valuable as your highest fee.

There is also the ethical dilemma of providing equal services to all your clients regardless of the compensation. Suppose your highest fee is $120 per hour, and your lowest is $50 per hour. Can you honestly say that you would provide the same quality service for the $50 client that you would provide for the $120 client? Even though you might make a conscious effort to do so, can you say with 100% certainty that you wouldn't unconsciously treat the $120 client better simply because they're paying more?

Finally there is the issue of fairness. Suppose you were a patient at a therapist's office that offered a sliding fee scale. Because of your income, you're expected to pay $120 per session. Further suppose your next-door neighbor is also a patient at the same therapist's office, but due to his income, he is only required to pay $50 per session. Are you going to think that it is fair that you have to pay more than he does? If you really want to be fair to all of your clients, you'll have to charge them all the same price. If you reduce your fee for one client, you'll eventually have to reduce your fee for all clients, or you won't be in business for long.

Insurance Panels: The Basics

In this chapter we'll focus primarily on insurance panels. Chapter 5 will deal with Employee Assistance Programs (EAPs) and Health Maintenance Organizations (HMOs).

An insurance panel is a group of providers authorized to be 'in network' on a particular insurance company's plan. What this means is that if you are on an insurance panel, you are an authorized provider for that insurance company. Once you are on the provider list for that insurance company, your name goes onto their website. When potential clients search for therapists in their area, a list of nearby approved providers pops up. If the insurance panel's website is a good one, the client will be able to click on a link that takes them to provider profiles. These profiles generally give information about the provider's specialties, preferred demographics, training and experience, hours and location. The potential client is able to compare therapists and choose one that most closely matches their needs. Most insurance companies are also moving to some method of evaluating therapists based on client satisfaction. If your insurance panel does this, then your provider profile may also have your client satisfaction rating listed with your other information, so potential clients can compare outcome evaluations among various therapists.

Once you have been accepted to an insurance panel, you may also mention this fact in any promotional materials associated with your private practice. This can be especially helpful information to include on brochures and on your website so that potential clients know immediately whether or not you accept their brand of insurance.

When the client contacts you and schedules an appointment, you will have to do a pre-authorization. What this means is that you will contact the insurance company on the client's behalf to pre-authorize therapy services. While not all insurance policies require pre-authorization for all services, it is best practice to do a pre-authorization for all new patients. Here's why: If your new patient has a policy that does not require pre-authorization for some services, but does require pre-authorization for other services, you will have no way of knowing which services may be covered and which servicers may not be unless you read each new patient's policy in depth. The only way to know for sure is to do a pre-authorization.

Let's say your new patient is coming to you for depression. You run an Explanation of Benefits (EOB) report with the patient's insurance company, and the insurance representative tells you that no pre-authorization is required for treatment for depression. So you don't run a pre-authorization. You do an assessment on the patient and discover that the diagnosis is actually Bipolar Disorder and not depression, so you send in your monthly billing with that diagnosis instead. If the patient's insurance policy covers depression without pre-authorization, but requires pre-authorization for treatment for Bipolar Disorder, the claim will be rejected. This means that if you intend to be paid, you will now have to either file an appeal with the insurance company, or send a bill to the client. If you choose the latter option, be aware that the majority of clients won't be angry at the insurance company for denying payment. They will be angry with you for not filing a pre-authorization, even though you were under the impression that one wasn't necessary.

When filing a pre-authorization the insurance company will ask you to provide a preliminary diagnosis. In most cases where a pre-authorization is filed, you have not yet met the patient. The patient calls you to schedule an appointment, giving you a presenting problem. You then contact the insurance company to find out if they're going to pay you before scheduling the first appointment with the client. If you don't do a pre-authorization before scheduling the first appointment, you run the risk of not being paid for the first appointment. So what this means is that the pre-authorization must be completed before you've met the patient face-to-face. This creates an ethical quandary for the therapist, because the insurance company is asking you to diagnose someone you've never met.

Nonetheless, if you intend to be paid for your services, it is necessary to run a pre-authorization on all patients, even if their policy states that pre-authorization isn't necessary. This means that you will have to come up with some sort of preliminary provisional diagnosis for the pre-authorization. Be aware that if, once you meet with the client, your diagnosis changes, the pre-authorization may be invalid and the insurance company may not pay for the new diagnosis.

When you are seeing the client on a regular basis, the insurance company will tell you how many authorized visits are allowed, what the client's co-pay will be, and what diagnoses are reimbursable. You will then send the insurance company a monthly 'superbill' for payment. The standard forms used for this are the HCFA 1500 or the CMS 1500. This is a standardized form used by all insurance companies. You may also purchase software that will allow you to complete and file these forms electronically. A more in-depth discussion of the billing process follows later in this chapter.

If your claim is denied for any reason, you have the right to appeal the denial. If your appeal is denied, you are required to abide by the insurance company's decision. Some companies allow you to bill your patients for any denied claims, while others do not. If you are on an insurance panel that does not allow you to bill your clients for any unpaid balances due to rejected claims by the insurance company, you have no further recourse for payment. This is why it is imperative that you read your insurance company's contract and make sure you understand it before signing.

In-Network vs. Out-of-Network

Once you have applied and are accepted to an insurance company's panel, you are considered to be 'in-network.' This means that you are an approved provider within that particular insurance company. If you are not on an insurance company's panel, you are 'out-of-network.' Insurance companies give preferential treatment to therapists who are in their network, but out-of-network status does not automatically bar you from getting paid.

If a patient has a type of insurance that you do not accept; that is, an insurance that you're not on the panel for, you can apply for out-of-network benefits for that patient's insurance. While it is rare that an insurance company will pay a provider not on their network, it's not unheard of. Some situations in which they might be willing to authorize payment would be the following:

- If you have an area of expertise that no one else on their panel has (For example, if your specialty is schizophrenia, and no other providers on their network offer expertise in treating schizophrenia)
- If your patient has special needs that might be served by your particular skills or orientation (For example, your treatment orientation is Solution-Focused Therapy, and the client prefers a Solution-Focused approach)
- If your patient has used you in the past or is familiar with your reputation and wishes to come to you as opposed to another therapist with your skills and training

Some beginning therapists think that they would like to simply apply for out-of-network benefits for all of their patients, and forego the time and trouble of applying to insurance panels. The problem with this is that while out-of-network benefits are occasionally granted by insurance companies in rare instances, such opportunities are few and far between. They are enough of a rarity that it would be impossible to sustain a private practice solely on out-of-network benefits.

National Provider Identification Number (NPI)

Before you begin to apply to insurance panels, you will need a National Provider Identification Number (NPI). A National Provider Identifier or NPI is a unique 10-digit identification number issued to health care providers in the United States by the Centers for Medicare and Medicaid Services (CMS). The NPI number is used to identify you or your practice in all transactions with insurance companies and other third party payers. It must be used in all electronic transactions identified by the Health Insurance Portability and Accountability Act (HIPAA) of 1996. The NPI may also be used in several other ways, including:

- To identify health care providers in non-electronic transactions (written correspondence)
- To identify health care providers for purposes of referral (For example, if you refer a patient to a psychiatrist)

- To identify yourself to insurance companies and other third party payers for purposes of payment
- By your insurance company to identify you to another insurance company, health care organization, or provider
- In communication between health care providers
- By health care clearinghouses to identify providers when processing transactions
- To identify providers in electronic patient records
- To cross reference providers in fraud and abuse cases being investigated by the Department of Health and Human Services
- For any other health care transaction requiring unique identification of a provider

When you apply to insurance panels, the application will ask you for your NPI number, so you will need to have one before you begin to apply. The NPI is also used on CMS 1500, HCFA 1500, and most EAP billing and invoices as your unique identifier. Think of it as a Social Security number for health care providers. It is unique to you, and it is used to distinguish you from any other health care provider. When you fill out your billing forms for insurance companies, EAPs and HMOs, this unique number will identify you to your third party payers so the funds go to the right person.

As an individual provider, you may have your own NPI number. If you are part of a clinic or other group practice, your organization may also have its own NPI number. If you are using an NPI number on billing, then if you use an individual number the payment will come to you. If you are using an NPI number that has been assigned to a group, then the payment will come to the group.

It's a simple matter to apply for a National Provider Identifier (NPI) Number online. It only takes a few minutes. To apply for an NPI number, visit https://nppes.cms.hhs.gov.

Soliciting Insurance Panels

To begin the process of applying to insurance panels, you would first send a letter of inquiry asking if they are accepting new clinicians with your expertise, and in your geographical area. In your letter of inquiry, be sure to include the following information:

- A brief outline of your training and experience. You do not have to include a resume or CV, as this will be included in your application packet if they are accepting new clinicians. Take special care to emphasize any unique training that might set you apart from other clinicians in your area.
- What sort of clients you are seeking. Do you have a preferred demographic or a preferred diagnosis?

- A statement of how long you have been licensed.
- A statement of why you think this insurance company should allow you on its panel.
- A statement of why you want to be on this insurance company's panel.

If the insurance company is interested in you, they will either send you an application package, or they will send you a letter telling you where to find their online application.

Different types of insurance have different standards for acceptance to their panels. Some require three years of post-graduate experience before accepting you. Others require three years of post-licensure experience. Some will accept you as soon as you are licensed. Some will waive their standards (within limits) if they have a need for someone with your expertise.

A key component of getting on insurance panels is whether or not the market is saturated in your area. What this means is that most insurance companies will only accept a certain amount of clinicians in a given zip code. The reason for this is that if there are too many therapists on the same insurance panel in a given area, then those therapists are likely to starve. While it may seem counterintuitive to think that insurance companies would turn down therapists, once the market becomes saturated many panels no longer accept new providers. It would seem that the more therapists an insurance company has, the more choices their clients would have, but in reality it is a buyer's market. If a region is saturated with therapists, insurance companies can pick and choose the top clinicians out of that larger pool. This means that their customers are more likely to get better service.

If you are rejected the first time you apply, don't give up. Vacancies often open up. There is a lot of turnover on insurance panels, so if you apply frequently, you are more likely to be accepted. If you have been rejected several times, there is still hope. First, find a client who carries the insurance you're targeting. Next, have them send a letter to the insurance company explaining why they would like you to be accepted. You will also send your own letter explaining why you would like to be on their panel. If the client in question has insurance through their place of employment, send a copy of both your letter and the client's letter to the benefits manager for their employer. In your letter, outline your credentials, qualifications, and why you think you should be accepted onto their panel. Have the client state why they were referred to you, and why they would like to see you. Have the client sign a release of information before sending their letter, and send a copy of the release as well.

Once an insurance panel has expressed an interest in you, they will send you an application. Although standards vary from one insurance company

to the next, most of them will want, at minimum, the following information:
- A copy of your license
- A copy of your resume or CV
- Transcripts from your graduate school
- A copy of your liability insurance information and/or certificate of insurance
- Information about your preferred treatment models/training
- Copies of all of your certificates and training
- Information about your preferred demographic
- Information about your preferred diagnoses
- A statement that you agree to their fee structure

On average it takes about three months for an insurance panel to make a decision regarding your application. If accepted, they will usually send you a letter or an email to that effect, but not always. I once applied to an insurance company and waited several months to hear from them. I never got a letter or email telling me I had been accepted. What I did get was a referral. When I told the client I wasn't on their insurance panel, her response was, "That's funny…they referred me to you."

So I went to that company's website and searched their list of providers. Sure enough, I was listed among them. I had been accepted, but they neglected to inform me of the fact. So if you have applied to a company and you haven't heard from them after a few weeks, it's a good idea to check in with them from time to time.

Coalition for Affordable Quality Healthcare (CAQH)

The average insurance panel application is around 30 pages long, and the average Marriage and Family Therapist is on at least five insurance panels. Needless to say, it can be quite tedious to send the same information over and over again to difference insurance companies. That's where CAQH comes in.

'CAQH' stands for the Coalition for Affordable Quality Healthcare. One of its primary services is to be a clearing house for credentialing for mental health professionals and other health care service providers. As you apply to insurance panels, Employee Assistance Programs, and Health Maintenance Organizations, it can become tedious and expensive to send the same information over and over again to various third party providers. CAQH takes your credentialing information and stores it in a central database. They then assign you a 'CAQH Number.' If you are applying to a third party payer who uses CAQH to check your credentials, all you have to do is give that agency your CAQH number. They can then go onto the CAQH website and download your credentials. CAQH verifies your credentials ahead of time, and they require periodic updating of your credentialing file. So any third party payer who looks at your CAQH file knows that they are getting up-to-date, verified information.

There will be an in-depth discussion of how CAQH works and how to apply for a CAQH account in Chapter 5.

Billing

In order to bill insurance companies you will either need to engage the services of a medical billing agency or do it yourself. I have done it both ways, and if you have access to a professional, I'd recommend hiring them to do your billing for you. Each insurance company has different standards for billing, and those standards are always changing. Each agency and each individual family's policy will also have different criteria for payment, and rather than having to learn all of this yourself, it is simply easier to pay a professional. When I was doing my own billing, I was spending an average of two hours of time on insurance paperwork, telephone calls, and appeals for every hour of client contact. As a self-employed private practitioner you're already going to have huge demands on your time, so it's probably well worth it to hire someone. Medical billers usually charge an enrollment fee of between $100 and $300 in order to add you to their billing software, then a percentage of any claims paid (usually between 5% and 10%). The enrollment fee is used to pay any fees associated with enrolling you in their electronic billing programs.

If you decide to do your own billing, you will need to either file by paper claims, or online. Be aware that insurance companies are not making any money by paying claims, so their online processes are purposefully designed to be confusing. Whether by design or by accident, much of the billing information on insurance websites is also inaccurate. That's why most medical billing companies file using paper claims. The forms most often used for 'superbills' are the CMS 1500 and the HCFA 1500. You can purchase software for your computer that will fill these forms out for you automatically, or you may request copies of the forms from your insurance company. Since different therapy practices have different needs, it is beyond the scope of this book to discuss how to fill out these forms. Insurance providers occasionally offer seminars on filling out these forms, so check with your agencies to see when you might be able to attend one. In some cases, you might even be able to obtain continuing education credit for such seminars.

In general, when a client wishes to use insurance, there will be a client co-pay and a portion that the insurance company pays. Be aware that most insurance companies pay about half of what fair market value is for a therapy session. In my region, the fair market value of an hour of therapy is around $120, and most insurance companies and EAPs pay about $60 per hour. You don't get to tell the insurance companies what your rate is. They tell you what they're willing to pay, and you can take it or leave it.

In addition to the client's co-pay, there is a deductible to be met. Not all insurance policies have deductibles, but most of them do. Over the years I've been in practice, those deductibles have gotten larger and larger. Deductibles of between $500 and $1500 are routine for most behavioral health policies, and these deductibles 'roll over' at the beginning of the year. What this means is that most policies re-set on January 1. So for example, if your patient has a deductible of $500, and they start seeing you later in the year, and by December 31 their deductible hasn't been met yet, then as of January 1 the deductible becomes $500 again and they have to start all over.

If a patient has a deductible, then they would pay your full contracted fee until the deductible is met, then they would pay their co-pay or co-insurance for any sessions after the deductible is met. Your contracted fee with their insurance company is the fee that the insurance company has told you they will pay you. It is not your standard fee. For example, let's say you have a standard fee of $120. This is the fee that someone walking in off the street without insurance would pay out-of-pocket. Let's assume you are also on an insurance panel that has told you that they will pay you $60 per hour for your services. If a client of yours has that particular insurance, and they have a deductible that hasn't been met yet, then you can only charge them the $60 contracted rate per one-hour session, and not your established standard rate of $120.

So let's say that you have a new patient. We'll call him 'Joe.' Joe has a policy with Insurance Company X. You're on Insurance Company X's panel, so Joe schedules his first appointment with you in the first week of January. You run an Explanation of Benefits and a pre-authorization on Joe's policy and discover that he has a deductible of $1500. Your contracted rate with Insurance Company X is $60 per hour, and they will only pay for one session per week with Joe. This means that your new patient's deductible will not be met until after 25 sessions! Joe will have to pay the full $60 per session until the deductible is met. Once the full $1500 has been met, then Joe will go to paying his co-pay and/or co-insurance for the remaining sessions. Note that a period of 25 sessions at one session per week is approximately six months long, and deductibles roll over in January of every year. So if Joe started seeing you after June of a given year, his deductible would not be met before it rolled over again on January 1. This means that Joe would always be paying your contracted rate of $60 per hour without ever meeting his deductible.

Let's assume that Joe has met his deductible and will be paying only a co-pay for the rest of his visits until his deductible rolls over at the end of the year. The average co-pay is between $15 and $30. Joe's co-pay is $30. This means that, once Joe's deductible has been met, he will pay $30 per visit for any remaining visits, and you will bill the insurance company for the balance. If your contracted rate with Joe's insurance company is $60 per session, and Joe's co-pay is $30, this means that you will be billing the insurance company for $30 per session with Joe. Most insurance companies only allow billing on a monthly basis, so this means that by the end of the month Joe will have paid, at most, $120 for four weekly sessions, and the insurance company owes you a balance of $120. Once you bill the company, it usually takes between thirty and ninety days to get reimbursed. So you will be carrying a deficit of $120, owed by the insurance company, until they decide to pay you.

Also be aware that insurance companies can deny a claim for any reason, and they don't always tell you ahead of time that a claim will be denied. So if you have seen Joe for a month, and then send a bill to the insurance company, and then they take a month to respond, they could deny the claim. By this time, if Joe is coming regularly, you will have seen him for two consecutive months, or eight sessions total. Clients generally aren't happy if you come to them after eight or more sessions and tell them that their insurance has denied their claim, but there is no way around this. Even if you have pre-authorization stating that they will pay the claim, they don't always go by this agreement. Your only recourse is to either bill Joe for your time, or appeal to the insurance company and ask them to reconsider their decision. Some insurance companies won't even allow you to bill the client for denied claims, so if that happens, you're just out the money for the sessions.

Whatever you do, don't send a client a bill for denied insurance claims if their insurance company doesn't allow you to do that. And never send a bill for the balance between your customary fee and your insurance company's contracted rate. To do either of these could constitute insurance fraud and could lead you not only to the loss of your license, but also possible prosecution for criminal charges.

Co-Pays and Co-Insurance

Usually clients have to pay a co-pay once their deductible is met, but sometimes they may have to pay a co-insurance instead. In some cases they may even have to pay both.

A co-pay is a flat fee that your clients pay after they've met their deductible, if any. Co-pays are usually listed on the back of the client's insurance card, but not always. Be aware that sometimes the co-pay is different for behavioral health services than it would be for a medical office visit.

Co-insurance is a percentage that is paid for any services received. This is an out-of-pocket expense that the client pays after meeting the deductible.

It's rare that your clients would have to pay both a co-pay and a co-insurance, but it's not totally unheard of. It usually occurs when there are multiple services on the same bill. For example, assessments are generally billed under a different CPT code than regular office visits, and most insurance companies will only pay for one assessment visit, so your client might have a co-pay for the assessment visit, then a co-insurance percentage fee for regular treatment visits. When in doubt about whether your client owes co-pay or co-insurance fees, check with the Explanation of Benefits (EOB) report or the Preauthorization Report.

Disadvantages and Pitfalls of Accepting Insurance

There are quite a few disadvantages to accepting insurance. Insurance companies are frustrating, confusing, and bewildering. Unfortunately, the only alternative to accepting insurance is to try to open an out-of-pocket, fee-for service business, and new therapists rarely have the reputation or marketing skills to succeed in such a business model. It's hard enough making a living as a therapist if you do take insurance. So consider the material in this section for information purposes, under the idea of 'forewarned is forearmed.'

The first disadvantage of insurance companies is that they can deny a claim for any reason. They will even sometimes deny claims even though they preauthorized payment before services were rendered. This usually happens because insurance companies require a preliminary diagnosis when you apply for preauthorization. The problem with requiring a preliminary diagnosis for preauthorization is that you are usually being asked to diagnose a client you haven't met face-to-face yet. In other words, you're just speculating on the diagnosis when you apply for preauthorization. So if you then see the client, do an assessment, and discover that they have a different diagnosis than what you put on the preauthorization, the claim could be denied because the client has a diagnosis for which treatment is not covered.

Another issue with insurance companies is client confidentiality and privacy. Most insurance companies require a diagnosis in order to pay for treatment. This diagnosis becomes part of your patient's permanent medical and behavioral health history. Although it is supposed to be illegal and unethical for businesses and schools to use such information against your clients, it has happened in the past. Witness the recent controversy over several school shootings in which the shooter's behavioral health history was revealed to the public, and you can see why this might be a privacy concern.

Deductibles and co-payments for mental health services are often high, as noted earlier in this section. The Affordable Care Act may address this issue as more components of that law come online, but currently deductibles range from $500 to $1500 for behavioral health services. At the average insurance remittance of around $60 per session, a $500 deductible would be met after 9 sessions, and a $1500 would not be met until after the 25th session! Clients tend to become frustrated when they discover that their insurance coverage isn't optimal, so it's imperative that you have a talk with each insurance client early on in the treatment process to go over their insurance benefits. If you haven't explained benefits to the client in detail, they won't become frustrated with their insurance companies if payment is denied. They'll be frustrated with *you*.

During your insurance briefing with new patients, you will want to explain their deductibles, co-pays, co-insurance, and your policy on payment for denied claims. If your client's insurance panel doesn't allow you to bill the client for denied claims, you may want to explain this to them. In addition to your explanation of coverage and benefits, may will to cover the following topics and explain them in detail to your new patient:

- Some services may not be covered.
- Axis II diagnoses (Personality Disorders) are rarely covered.
- Insurance adjusters often make treatment decisions based on their definition of 'medical necessity,' and not the therapist's, or the patient's.
- This means that in most cases an insurance claims manager who has never met your patients face-to-face is making medical decisions on their health care.
- Insurance companies usually offer a limited number of sessions (usually between 5 and 12).
- If treatment is still needed after the approved number of sessions, you or your patient must re-apply for authorization for more sessions.
- Marriage and relationship counseling is rarely covered unless one or both partners has a diagnosable Axis I disorder in addition to marital problems.
- Insurance companies rarely, if ever, pay for V-code diagnoses. Many marital problems fall into this category, so if you are doing marital therapy, insurance companies probably won't pay you for this service unless there is also an Axis I diagnosis.
- If your patients get their behavioral health insurance through their employer and the employer pays a portion of the cost, their employer may have a legal right to check into their records.
- Insurance companies may have a legal right to know everything about the care your patients receive, depending on terms of the insurance contract.

- Confidentiality is difficult to maintain during the insurance billing process and anyone who works for the insurance company may have access to your patient's information. This is one of the reasons that the Health Insurance Privacy and Accountability Act, or HIPAA, was created in the first place.
- When behavioral health providers agree to join an insurance panel, they agree to follow all of that company's insurance guidelines. This means the provider is restricted by the insurance company's recommendations as to the type of therapy used, the amount of sessions provided, the length of the sessions, and in some cases, the number of people present during sessions.
- Not all insurance companies will pay for family therapy, which is billed under a different CPT code than individual therapy.
- In most cases the only way to determine for sure if the claim will be paid, is to submit a claim for services already rendered.
- If they deny the claim, and don't allow you to bill the patient, you're just out the money for services provided.
- If the therapist believes one therapy is best for the client and the insurance disagrees, the client gets the therapy chosen by the insurance company, and not by the therapist. Either that, or the insurance company won't pay for treatment.
- Most deductibles roll over after the first of the year, so there is a great deal of patient attrition in January through March (there is also a rush in October through December of patients trying to get sessions in before their deductibles roll over).
- If you forget to account for this attrition rate at the first of the year, and if a high volume of your business is with insurance companies, you can be put in severe financial difficulties at this time of year.
- Insurance regulations usually change on January 1 too, so there is usually a crunch to become familiar with the new regulations. This is especially true if you do your own billing.
- Insurance companies are notorious for making it extremely difficult to find information on properly filing claims.
- Insurance companies can audit your files at any time.
- If your records are not up to the insurance company's standards, or if they find any problems with the treatment you provided, then they can require you to pay back any remittances for services provided.

Obviously there are a lot of disadvantages to working with insurance companies. Unfortunately, they hold all the cards at present, so if you plan to make it as a private practice therapist, there's not much of an alternative.

In addition to the above cautions about working with insurance companies, there are a few other items of which you should be aware. Due to a surplus of counselors and therapists on the market in most regions, many of the bigger companies aren't taking any new providers. This is especially true in urban centers and bigger cities. The few companies that are taking new providers are generally increasing their standards for provider credentials. Many now require three to five years of post-graduate experience before they will accept your application to sit on their insurance panel. Some even require three to five years of *post-licensure* experience before accepting you as a provider.

You should also be aware of the fact that even if an insurance company accepts you to serve on their panel, this is not an automatic guarantee of referrals from that company. I've been on some insurance panels for five years without a single referral. Don't rely on the insurance companies to send people your way. The best way to get new clients is to go out and solicit them yourself. The best way to do this is to go and introduce yourself to local doctor's offices, hospitals, community agencies, and mental health organizations that accept that company's insurance.

The Affordable Care Act and Mental Health

As this book is being written, we are very close to full implementation of the Affordable Care Act, also known as 'Obamacare.' How will the Affordable Care Act (ACA) impact the mental health professions? Will it help or hinder those who are starting a private practice?

The first thing to remember about the ACA is that it is not a health care law. It is a health insurance law. Provisions of the law will govern how insurance companies do business with their clients. The provisions do not do anything to interfere with how doctors and therapists provide care to patients.

According to research, one of the chief reasons that people do not seek behavioral health treatment is a lack of insurance coverage. The ACA will allow most people who are now uninsured to get affordable health care insurance. This insurance will also cover behavioral health treatment. When the ACA is fully implemented, over 90% of Americans will have health insurance of some sort. People who cannot otherwise afford health insurance will receive subsidies that will help them to pay most of the costs of coverage. In states that haven't opted out of the Medicaid expansion, more people will be eligible for Medicaid. This expansion will also allow low-income, single adults with no children to enroll in Medicaid for the first time.

The ACA also provides for coverage of mental health and substance abuse service, and sets standards of care for such coverage. Preventative care is a priority, and the law addresses inefficiencies in the current behavioral health care system and provides for quality control and improvement of delivery of services.

Many people who have psychiatric disorders are covered by public programs such as Medicaid and Medicare. The ACA makes it easier for many of these people to get insurance through private companies instead of relying on public programs. Currently, about 90% of people with serious mental illnesses are unemployed. This means that they do not have access to employer-based insurance plans, and must rely on public assistance. Before ACA, insurance companies could deny coverage based on a person's mental health or lack thereof. Prior to ACA, insurance companies could also deny coverage for pre-existing conditions. They could also cap payments for ongoing treatment. This means that once your policy's limit had been reached, they could terminate your benefits whether you were well or not.

The Affordable Care Act addresses all of these issues. Under ACA's "guaranteed issue and renewal" provision, insurance companies have to sell policies to all who apply. They also have to renew all policies for all who apply for renewal. If the old policy doesn't offer coverage mandated by ACA, a new policy will be issued with the updated coverage. Insurers can no longer deny coverage for pre-existing conditions, and can no longer issue a lifetime limit on benefits. They are also forbidden under ACA to charge people in poor health more than they would charge healthy people. Health insurance companies, under ACA, will no longer be able to discriminate against clients based on a physical or mental disability. Young adults 26 years of age or younger may also remain on their parents' health plans if the parents so desire.

One provision of the law that some people see as a drawback is that it will require all people to carry health insurance. What some fail to understand is that if you cannot afford health insurance, the ACA will supplement your health care coverage so that your insurance will be affordable. This mandate for health insurance is not much different than the mandate in most states that drivers carry automobile insurance. The individual mandate means that taxpayers aren't stuck paying for emergency room health care for those without the oversight and responsibility to have health insurance.

The Medicaid expansion will mean more access to community services for those with mental health issues. These services include skills training, employment assistance and training, housing assistance, therapy, and medication coverage. The Medicaid package of services is much broader than the typical insurance plan's bundle of services. Because of this, Medicaid is often the better option for people with psychiatric disorders.

Under the Affordable Care Act, anyone below 133% of the federal income poverty level will be eligible for Medicaid beginning in 2014. Some groups will be eligible sooner than that. States are required to keep their current Medicaid eligibility rules until 2014 for adults and 2019 for children in order to prevent states from removing people from the Medicaid rolls when the new coverage requirements begin.

Another feature of the ACA is that insurance companies and Medicaid/Medicare must achieve parity between mental and physical health issues. This means that limits cannot be placed on medically necessary mental health and substance abuse treatment. The jury is still out on what constitutes 'medically necessary' and who determines this.

In order to make it easier for consumers to compare advantages and disadvantages of various health care plans, the Affordable Care Act establishes state-based health markets called 'Exchanges.' The law states that these exchanges must be established by January 1, 2014, and beginning in 2017 large employers may also use the exchanges to purchase health insurance. Exchanges act as middlemen, allowing consumers to compare various policies and pick the best one for their needs. The exchanges will have the effect of increasing competition between insurance markets, and thereby lowering the cost to consumers.

All insurance plans that participate in the exchanges will have to meet certain criteria, including providing coverage for mental health and substance abuse treatment. All plans participating in the exchanges must offer a range of services determined by the federal government. In addition to mental health and substance abuse treatment, such plans must include coverage for rehabilitative services, hospitalizations, emergency room services, prescription drugs, and preventive services/wellness programs. This is of great benefit to behavioral health consumers, because it means that any plan that they purchase through an exchange will have coverage for behavioral health treatments.

The Affordable Care Act also establishes grants that will be used to expand existing insurance assistance, and to create new assistance programs. Such assistance programs will help customers enroll in plans, fill out paperwork, evaluate various plans, and file complaints and appeals. These offices will also educate the public on their rights and responsibilities under the Affordable Care Act.

The ACA establishes an integrated approach to behavioral health by creating health care homes for people with chronic conditions. These homes will provide comprehensive case management and long-term care. They are also mandated to work with community support agencies to provide the best possible care. This is good news for any private practitioner willing to accept referrals from such homes.

The Affordable Care Act also establishes $50 million in grant money from the Substance Abuse and Mental Health Services Administration for establishing on-site treatment in such home care facilities. These programs are also mandated to be as integrated as possible, relying on a community support model for the provision of behavioral health and substance abuse services. The law establishes Community Health Teams to address these issues. Such teams would include primary health care providers, including behavioral health care providers. The ultimate goal is to provide person-centered treatment using a community team approach.

The Affordable Care Act will also make prescription drugs more affordable. This includes psychotropic drugs routinely used in mental health. The law makes it easier to purchase some drugs, such as benzodiazapines and barbiturates. The law will also streamline the process of applying for Medicaid programs so that people with psychiatric disorders will feel less intimidated when applying for services.

Other quality improvement provisions of the Affordable Care Act include:

- Establishment of the Centers for excellence in depression treatment
- Funding for research, screening, education and treatment of postpartum depression
- Establishment of grants for the purpose of promoting positive health behaviors
- Encouragement of integrated services
- Encouragement of a person-centered approach to therapy
- Promotion of interdisciplinary training of all health care professionals, including mental health professionals

Mental health disorders are the leading cause of disability for people between the ages of 15 and 44. Mental disorders, including substance abuse disorders, are also a significant cause of lost productivity in the workplace. These provisions in the Affordable Care Act will be a first step in addressing the dire need for effective and comprehensive behavioral health care in America.

A Note on Liability Insurance

You've worked hard up to this point to establish yourself as a mental health professional. You don't want to lose it all due to a lawsuit, so you're going to need liability insurance. There are two major types of liability insurance: Malpractice insurance and slip-and-fall coverage.

Malpractice insurance protects you from lawsuits against your practice for some sort of injury to your patients. Such coverage is not only a good idea; it's also mandatory if you plan to be on most insurance panels and third party payers. They're going to require that you carry malpractice insurance before they're willing to accept you on their panels. You'll be required to show proof of insurance every year at re-credentialing time with your insurance panels, EAPs, and HMOs. If you are registered with the Coalition for Quality Affordable Healthcare (CAQH), you will also have to update your insurance information with them on an annual basis.

How much coverage should you purchase? The current industry standard recommended minimum is $1 million individual and $3 million aggregate. The $1 million individual covers your personal liability in case of a lawsuit, and the $3 million aggregate covers everything else. The $1 million - $3 million standard is the minimum most insurance companies will accept for malpractice coverage if you intend to be on their panels. If you purchase less coverage, you may be denied access to some of the larger insurance companies. Some are even moving to a higher $2 million individual and $5 million aggregate coverage for their providers. If you can afford it, more coverage is always preferable to less.

The next primary type of liability insurance is a slip-and-fall policy. It protects you from everything your malpractice insurance doesn't. If someone trips down the stairs of your office, or if a tree falls on their car in the parking lot, or if any other accident or 'acts of God' occur while your patients are in your office, this policy should cover your liability. If you are renting office space instead of buying, most landlords will require you to purchase some sort of slip-and-fall policy. Some may even require that you carry the landlord as an additional insured, so that they are also protected should one of your patients sue.

You might also consider renter's insurance, in case a fire or other natural disaster destroys your office, or in case of theft, but at bare minimum you will definitely need malpractice insurance and a slip-and-fall policy. Discuss your needs with your insurance agent. If you don't currently have an insurance agent, ask someone you trust for a recommendation. Ideally you should have your insurance policies in place before you open the door on your first day of private practice.

5 EAPs and HMOs

Many medium-to-large businesses offer Employee Assistance Program (EAP) services to employees. As more components of the Affordable Care Act come online, even more small businesses may begin to offer employee assistance programs for behavioral health services, as the ACA requires parity for behavioral health treatment, and offering EAP services for mental health is one way to accomplish this goal.

In general, Employee Assistance Programs (EAPs) charge businesses a subscriber fee for each employee to contract for behavioral health (and other health) services. These services are usually free to employees as a part of their benefits package.

Since services are usually free to employees, EAPs are generally an attractive part of any benefits package. While they usually only offer a limited number of sessions (from three to five sessions is customary), the employee has the option of continuing on an out-of-pocket basis if the issue hasn't been resolved by the time the approved sessions have expired. If you are on the employee's insurance panel, you may also begin to bill their regular insurance once their EAP benefits have been used.

Since EAP services are usually free to employees, they are more likely to use these benefits than their insurance, which may have a co-pay or co-insurance. And since the EAP pre-approves any patients they send your way, you know ahead of time that you'll get paid for the pre-approved sessions, so there's no wrestling with insurance companies for payment. Most EAPs just request that you send in an invoice once per month, and they send a check or a direct deposit for approved sessions.

Since the employer pays for EAP services, the utilization of EAP benefits is of lower cost to the employee. Research has demonstrated that companies that provide EAP services to their employees have lower rates of employee turnover and less employee absences. EAP services have also been correlated with higher employee productivity, so providing EAP services is a win-win situation for any company that chooses to do so.

If you choose to work heavily with Employee Assistance Programs, here are some statistics that you may find helpful:

- About 19.2 million U.S. workers (15%) reported using alcohol on the job or being intoxicated by alcohol while at work at least once in the previous year (Branham, 2008).
- By far the most expensive and frequent outpatient treatment for behavioral health for employees was substance abuse. Prevention programs have been shown to be far more cost effective than after-the-fact treatment, and companies that offer such services enjoy great savings in preventative care and employee productivity (Roman & Blum, 2002).
- Savings from investing in substance abuse treatment can exceed costs by a ratio of 12 to 1 (Bernstein & Mahoney, 1989).
- 217 million workdays per year are lost due to untreated mental disorders (Finch & Phillips, 2005).
- Depressed workers cost their companies an average of 5.6 productive hours per week, compared to an average loss of 1.5 hours per week for workers who are not depressed (Pilette, 2005).
- Workers with depression cost employers $44 billion per year in lost productivity (Stewart, et al 2003).
- Absence, disability and lost productivity related to mental illness cost employers more than four times the cost of employee medical treatment (*A Mentally Healthy Workplace - It's Good for Business*, 2006).

Obviously, companies that invest in Employee Assistance Programs reap many benefits over companies that do not offer such services.

If you are just starting out in private practice and don't have a lot of experience as a therapist or counselor, it may be difficult to get on an employee assistance program's provider panel. Many require at least three years of post-graduate experience as a therapist, and some are requiring three years of post-licensure experience. There was a trend towards Employee Assistance Programs requiring more experience, but the Affordable Care Act requires parity for behavioral health services, so that trend may change in the near future. Time will tell.

Another potential problem with getting on EAP panels is that the market is saturated in many areas. This means that in some areas (especially the more urban areas) there is a glut of providers. In those areas, some EAP panels may not be taking any more providers. It may help if you have a specialty that is not widely covered. For example, if you are trained in Play Therapy and there aren't any Play Therapy providers in your area, EAPs may be more interested in adding you to their panels.

If you are applying to Employee Assistance Programs, you should be aware that they have been criticized for their lack of impartiality in cases where an employee seeks assistance due to work-related issues. This means that since the employer is paying for the benefits, there tends to be a bias towards providing treatment that is quick and inexpensive, with the goal of getting the employee back to work as quickly as possible. While this might be possible for short term difficulties, disorders requiring longer treatments may be frowned upon. For example, an employee with a substance abuse problem is not likely to have much success in achieving recovery after only three to five sessions.

Programs where EAP providers are employed by the same company as the program participants are particularly criticized as being another arm of company management. In such a situation, the therapist or counselor is employed exclusively by the company to provide services to its employees. Such therapists usually have offices on the company's grounds, but they may sometimes operate out of an independent facility. In either case, if the therapist works exclusively for the company, employees tend to see that therapist as just another layer of management. Treatment in this case could be especially difficult if one of the employee's presenting problems is difficulty with management and/or authority figures on the job.

No matter how impartial the therapist strives to be, there is some truth to this criticism of 'working for the company, not the patient.' If your patients are referred by an EAP through their place of employment, most EAP provider contracts state that the therapist's primary responsibility is to the EAP, and not to the patient/client. What this means is that EAP contracts routinely ask you to put the needs of the company ahead of the needs of the patient. This puts the therapist in an ethical quandary, as a therapist's primary duty should be to the patient, and not to his or her employer. When signing a contract with an employee assistance program, make sure you understand what you're being asked to do, and that your duties as an EAP provider won't violate your ethical code and put your license in jeopardy. If necessary, have your attorney review the provider contract before signing it.

Another thing to be aware of with EAPs is that being approved for their panels doesn't automatically mean you will get referrals. You will still have to do a lot of self-promotion in order to get a steady stream of referrals from any EAP panel. Once accepted, you may wish to include this information on all of your promotional materials: Website, business cards, and brochures.

Applying to Employee Assistance Program Panels

The Coalition for Quality Affordable Healthcare (CAQH) is an organization that acts as a clearing house for provider credentials. Many Employee Assistance Programs use CAQH for verifying the credentials of providers who apply to be on their provider panels. The last section of this chapter will cover in detail what CAQH is and how to get your credentials listed with their database. Once you have a CAQH file, you will only need to give your CAQH number to any EAP panels that you are applying for, along with a brief application. The Employee Assistance Program panel application process is a relatively painless application procedure as opposed to the insurance panel application process.

The Certified Employee Assistance Professional (CEAP®) Credential

When compared with insurance panels, Employee Assistance Programs are much easier to work with. Since they approve sessions ahead of time, you know you will get paid. Their billing procedures and paperwork are also much easier, and many of them don't require a diagnosis in order to pay for treatment. Most of the EAPs I've worked with just ask whether or not there is any improvement from session to session.

If you plan to work a lot with EAPs, there is a credential you may wish to obtain that will put you ahead of the pack. The Certified Employee Assistance Professional (CEAP®) credential tells an EAP that you have training specific to their demographic. If you are a CEAP® you will get preferential treatment when EAPs refer clients.

There are three components to becoming a CEAP®: Work experience, continuing education, and advisement. You gain work experience by working specifically with patients who have been referred by employee assistance programs. The continuing education component includes classes and training in working specifically with clients referred by EAPs, and the advisement portion involves mentoring by a qualified professional trained in CEAP® advisement.

If you are interested in obtaining this credential, or would like more information, you may visit the Employee Assistance Program Association's website at http://www.eapassn.org or contact the certification committee's Certification Director at:

EACC
4350 North Fairfax Drive, Suite 410
Arlington, VA 22203
Fax: (703) 522-4585
Email: certdir@eapassn.org

Health Maintenance Organizations

A Health Maintenance Organization (HMO) is an organization that provides managed care, including behavioral health care, for health insurance, self-funded health care benefit plans, and individuals and acts as a liaison with health care providers (hospitals, doctors, etc.) on a prepaid basis. Customers 'subscribe' and pay a regular fee (usually monthly) to their HMO in exchange for health care benefits. A major difference between an EAP and an HMO is that in EAPs the business subscribes to the service and pays for the employee's EAP benefits, while in an HMO the individual subscribes to the service and pays the subscription fee for the benefits.

The theory behind HMOs is that there is a large pool of subscribers paying into the program, and only a certain percentage of those paying in will actually use the benefits at any given time, so those benefits are funded by the broad subscriber base. Although businesses originally pursued the HMO model for its alleged cost containment benefits, recent research indicates that private HMO plans don't achieve any significant cost savings over non-HMO plans. Because of this, many HMO plans have fallen out of favor with consumers.

Although out-of-pocket costs are reduced for consumers in HMO plans, the plans don't affect total expenditures and payments by insurers. Because of this, some have asserted that HMOs (especially those run for profit) actually increase administrative costs and tend to cherry-pick healthier patients so that they don't have to pay out as many benefits.

Applying to Health Maintenance Organization Panels

Since most Health Maintenance Organization panels are administered by insurance companies, the procedure for applying to be on an HMO panel is similar to the process of applying to be on an insurance panel. In fact, with some insurance companies, once you're accepted onto their panel you are also accepted onto their HMO, if they have one.

Many HMOs use CAQH for verifying provider credentials, so if you have a listing with CAQH, you would just fill out their panel application and give them your CAQH number for your credentials. For further details, contact the Provider Relations Department of a company that provides such services.

Coalition for Affordable Quality Healthcare (CAQH)

The Coalition for Affordable Quality Healthcare (CAQH) can be a tremendous help when applying to insurance panels, Employee Assistance Programs, and Health Maintenance Organizations.

Every time you apply to be on a provider panel, you have to send in your credentials so that the panel can verify that you are who you say you are and that you have the training you say you have. Not only that, but this information has to be updated annually as your trainings and experience change. If you are on multiple provider panels, you can see that it could be a major headache to constantly update your provider credentials with each company and to fill out multiple applications all containing the same information.

The Coalition for Affordable Quality Healthcare (CAQH) helps to alleviate this burden by acting as a clearinghouse for credentialing information. CAQH's Mission Statement is: *To be the catalyst for industry collaboration on initiatives that simplify healthcare administration for health plans and providers, resulting in a better care experience for patients and caregivers.*

CAQH's stated vision is: *A healthcare system in which administrative processes are efficient, predictable, and easily understood by patients, caregivers and providers. In this system, administrative and clinical data are integrated to effectively support the delivery of care.*

According to their website, the Coalition for Affordable Quality Healthcare (CAQH) is a nonprofit alliance of health plans and trade associations for simplifying healthcare administration through industry initiatives that promote quality interactions between plans, providers and other stakeholders, reduce costs and frustrations associated with healthcare administration, facilitate administrative healthcare information exchange, and encourage administrative and clinical data integration.

One of the ways CAQH accomplishes its mission and vision is to maintain provider files on all health care providers listed with their organization. Physicians, counselors, therapists, and other health care providers are now using CAQH for provider data collection. By creating a CAQH account, and submitting your credentials, your information is stored in a central location that is easily accessible to insurance panels, Employee Assistance Programs, and Health Maintenance Organizations. You only have to submit your credentials to one location, instead of to every insurance panel, HMO and EAP for which you apply.

How do I become a member of CAQH?

In order to create an account with CAQH, you must first apply to an insurance company, HMO or EAP that uses CAQH for credentialing purposes. To find out if a provider panel uses CAQH to verify credentials, either ask their Provider Relations Administrator or check the company's website for this information. Be sure to tell them, when applying for their panel, that you would also like to create a CAQH account.

When you submit your application, they will check with CAQH to see if you have an account. If you do not, they will ask CAQH to create an account for you. When this account has been created by CAQH, they will assign you a CAQH number for your account. When you get a CAQH number, you can create an account by logging on to the CAQH website at http://www.caqh.org.

When you have been issued a CAQH number and you have created your account, you will then upload all of your credentialing information to the CAQH website. They will then verify all of your credentials and create your account. Once your account is created, you can add insurance panels, EAPs, and HMOs to your account. There are two options for adding provider panels: You may either allow all panels access to your file, or you may choose the option of selecting individual companies as you apply to their panels and they request to view your credentials. If you choose this option, CAQH will send you an email when individual companies request permission to view your file, and then you will log on to the website and grant permission for the company to access your records. Because CAQH has already verified your credentials, individual provider panels don't have to do this, so the advantage of using CAQH is that they don't have to go to the time and expense of checking your credentials. The advantage to you is that you don't have to keep sending in your credentials to every panel you apply for. Once you have created your initial account, any other panels you apply for that use CAQH will only need your CAQH number in order to verify your credentials.

Once you've been accepted to a provider panel, you will need to create a Provider Profile on that company's website. Most insurance companies, EAPs and HMOs offer such a service so that their clients searching for a therapist can have access to information about your trainings, specialties, licensure and certification, and treatment orientation. You will need to update this Provider Profile periodically. It's a good idea to set a regular time to update all of your profiles for all of the provider panels you participate in. A good rule of thumb is that every time you complete a continuing education course or certification, you update all of your provider profiles. You may also wish to update all of your advertising materials in order to keep your patients current on which insurances, EAPs and HMOs you accept.

When you've been accepted to a new panel, immediately familiarize yourself with their billing procedures and policies. Even if you contract with a medical billing agency to handle your billing and invoices, it's still wise to have a basic understanding of billing procedures for each individual company, as well as your contractual obligations as a provider for that company. If there's a billing question at stake, your billing agency isn't liable for mistakes - you are! So be sure to know what your billing agent is doing on your behalf.

6 Professional Organizations

The professional organization for Family Therapists in the United States is the American Association of Marriage and Family Therapists (The AAMFT). If you are a licensed Marriage and Family Therapist and you are not a member of the AAMFT, this section discusses some of the benefits of joining, and some of the disadvantages. If you are another type of licensed behavioral health professional, we'll also look at some of the benefits of membership in other professional organizations as well.

Networking

If you are a member of the American Association of Marriage and Family Therapists, you have ample opportunities to meet others in the field. The biggest thing that sets Marriage and Family Therapy apart from other forms of psychotherapy is the fact that we have a completely unique treatment paradigm and philosophical underpinning based on the principles of Cybernetic Systems Theory. Because of this difference, being a member of the AAMFT allows you to interact with others who understand this philosophical difference and this treatment modality. There is a common frame of reference for all members of the AAMFT, so by being a member, you are assured that there are others who understand where you're coming from. This also means that you will have more access to and more information about continuing education opportunities based in this unique treatment philosophy.

Meeting with other Marriage and Family Therapists also gives you the opportunity to cross-refer with other members. Perhaps you specialize in Play Therapy, but not so much with couples. By networking with other Marriage and Family Therapists, you have the opportunity to seek referrals for Play Therapy, and the opportunity to refer couples to others who may focus on that particular demographic.

Another reason to join the American Association of Marriage and Family Therapists is for opportunities for peer supervision. If you are part of a network of Marriage and Family Therapists, you know that you can always reach out to others in the field if you need a consultation on a difficult case. Likewise, other members know that they may call upon your expertise.

Perhaps the most important advantage to networking with other Marriage and Family Therapists is the feeling of being part of something bigger. It's a great thing to know that you are part of an organization that supports you, your values, your experience and training.

Education

As was already mentioned, Marriage and Family Therapy is based on an entirely different theoretical modality than other forms of psychotherapy. Because of this, the educational requirements for Marriage and Family Therapists are completely different than for other therapists and counselors.

By joining the American Association of Marriage and Family Therapists, you are kept informed through magazines, journals, and email updates. *Family Therapy* magazine is published once every two months, and the Journal of Marriage and Family Therapy is a peer-reviewed clinical journal that is available online to members of the AAMFT. In addition to these publications, members of the AAMFT receive frequent email updates on events and educational opportunities at both the national and the state level. The AAMFT sponsors annual conferences at the national level. Continuing education opportunities are always available at these national conferences. In addition to the national conferences, all of the state organizations sponsor statewide annual conferences offering continuing education opportunities, and many states hold more than one conference per year.

The American Association of Marriage and Family Therapists also sponsors scholarship opportunities and maintains a database of Marriage and Family Therapy programs throughout the United States.

Intrinsic Value

Membership in the American Association of Marriage and Family Therapists as a clinical member offers you a provider profile through the Therapist Locator Network at http://www.therapistlocator.com. This means that people who use this service will have access to your private practice information if you take advantage of the opportunity to complete your profile.

Membership in the AAMFT also affords you discounts on seminars, continuing education seminars, educational materials, and conferences. Finally, in recent years the AAMFT has elected to open membership to people whose licensure may not be in Marriage and Family Therapy. This means that you can join as a clinical member even if your licensure is LPC, NCC, LISW, MISW, or some other category.

Disadvantages

Because the American Association of Marriage and Family Therapists is a newer organization, it is also smaller. One of the disadvantages of being a smaller organization is that there are fewer members paying dues, therefore our membership fees are about twice what many other professional organizations would pay.

Another potential disadvantage is that if you join the AAMFT you are agreeing to be bound by the ethical code of the American Association of Marriage and Family Therapists. This may not seem to be a disadvantage, but if the AAMFT's code is in conflict with your state's laws or the ethical codes of other organizations to which you belong, you could find yourself in an ethical or legal dilemma. Of course it goes without saying that a therapist should never want to do anything obviously unethical, but sometimes that line is not drawn so clearly.

For example, my practice is in South Carolina. According to South Carolina statutes, parents have the right to see anything in their minor child's case file at any time. Section 1.9 of the American Association of Marriage and Family Therapists' Code of Ethics says the following:

1.9 Relationship Beneficial to Client: *Marriage and family therapists continue therapeutic relationships only so long as it is reasonably clear that clients are benefiting from the relationship.*

Let's suppose I'm seeing a teenager who admits to having had sex with her boyfriend. The boyfriend is her age, so there's no reportable issue of statutory rape under South Carolina law. She admits to me in confidence that she has had sex with him, but hasn't told her parents because she is afraid of the repercussions. The child has disclosed this to me in confidence and confidentiality as her therapist. Now suppose one of the parents invokes their rights under South Carolina statutes to view the child's entire case file. They examine the file and discover that their daughter is having sex, and they punish her for it. Is this patient likely to ever trust me again with any information? In effect, the therapeutic relationship with this patient has been compromised, and ethically I should refer her to another therapist, because the therapeutic relationship is no longer beneficial to her.

Another potential disadvantage to membership in a professional organization is that you may be asked to volunteer to serve on committees or boards, or as an officer of the organization. Such positions are rarely paid positions, and they are often time-consuming. Of course any conscientious professional would want to give back to the profession in some way. Just be sure that you understand the time and work commitment before undertaking such positions. It's better to say "no" than it is to say "yes," and never show up for meetings or accomplish the tasks required for such positions. Above all, don't look at such opportunities as resume' fodder, but take the work seriously.

Other Professional Organizations

Since this book is geared primarily towards Marriage and Family Therapists, we've gone into more detail about the American Association of Marriage and Family Therapists (AAMFT). If you are a Marriage and Family Therapist, your state or province probably also has a state-level organization that you may wish to join. In many cases, membership in the American Association of Marriage and Family Therapists also automatically includes membership at the state level.

If you have another form of licensure or certification, or if you are interested in a particular subspecialty, there are some other professional organizations you may consider joining. Licensure as a Marriage and Family Therapist may make you eligible for some of these organizations, while other organizations may have different requirements. If in doubt, check with the organization.

Some of the benefits of joining any of the organizations listed below include:

- Professional Development: Membership in a group or subspecialty allows you to learn and grow as a therapist or counselor as you network with like-minded individuals.
- Potential reduced rates for CEUs and educational materials.
- Professional Identity: Membership in these organizations allows you to market yourself to key demographics. This is especially true if the organization is a subspecialty like Music Therapy, Art Therapy, etc. Such skills set you apart from other therapists and

counselors in your area who are not members of similar organizations.
- Newsletters: All of the organizations listed below offer newsletters to keep members informed of events, conferences, educational opportunities, and other happenings.
- Advocacy at the national and state levels: All of the organizations listed below advocate for members with third party payers, government agencies, and other health care professionals.
- Career opportunities: Most of the organizations listed below offer career centers to members. These career centers are usually based online, and offer listings of job openings for the organization's particular specialty.
- Free listing: Many of the organizations below offer some sort of free listing in their website, their newsletter, or other promotional materials. Such a listing recognizes you as a member of the organization and acknowledges to the general public that you have the skills taught by that organization.
- Code of Ethics: All of the organizations listed below have a Code of Ethics specific to the organization. This helps to clarify any potential gray areas when practicing under the auspices of the organization.

The following section contains membership information about each organization, along with contact information for becoming a member.

American Art Therapy Association

The American Art Therapy Association connects you to the important work of art therapists around the world who use the creative process to help people of all ages improve their health and emotional well-being. The Association represents more than 5,000 members around the world and in its 40 Chapters throughout the United States.

The American Art Therapy Association has several membership categories:
- Credentialed Professional - Individuals who maintain current registration (ATR) and/or certification (ATR-BC) through the Art Therapy Credentials Board, Inc. (ATCB). Credentialed Professional members shall be eligible to vote, hold office, serve on committees, and receive all official Association publications, and all other rights and benefits provided by the Association.
- Professional - Individuals who have completed graduate level training in art therapy. Applicants for Professional membership must provide proof of their graduate degree with their

application. Professional members shall have all the rights and privileges granted to Credentialed Professional members.
- New Professional - Individuals who have completed graduate level training in art therapy within the last twelve (12) months. New Professional membership is available for one year only and must be upgraded to Professional or Credentialed Professional in the second year. Applicants for New Professional Membership must provide proof of their graduate degree with their application. New Professional members shall have all the rights and privileges granted to Professional members.
- Student - Individuals who do not meet the qualifications of Professional membership and who are currently enrolled in institutions of higher learning and are interested in art therapy. Student members must currently be enrolled in an institution of higher learning and must provide a copy of their student ID. Student members have all the rights and privileges accorded student members of the Association as outlined on the membership benefits matrix, except they may not vote or hold office on the national level. Student members have access to the Journal electronically only.
- Student PLUS - Student PLUS members receive the same benefits as Students (above), PLUS: receive one year of Student Professional Liability Insurance, and a printed copy of Art Therapy: Journal of the American Art Therapy Association.
- Associate - Individuals interested in art therapy and who wish to support the purposes and objectives of the Association. This category is not open to individuals who have completed graduate level training in art therapy or are working as art therapists. Associate members shall have all the rights and privileges granted to Professional members of the Association, except they may not vote or hold office.
- Retired Professional - Professional and Credentialed Professional members who have reached the age of 65, or who are eligible to retire with full benefits under the current Social Security regulations, and are officially retired from their primary professional activities. Retired Members have all the rights and privileges granted to Credentialed or Professional members of the Association.
- Retired Associate - Associate members who have reached the age of 65, or who are eligible to retire with full benefits under the current Social Security regulations, and are officially retired from their primary professional activities. Retired Members

have all the rights and privileges granted to Credentialed or Professional members of the Association, except they may not vote or hold office.
- International - Individuals living outside of the United States who are working in the field of art therapy or are interested in art therapy and wish to support the purposes and objectives of the Association. International members shall have all the rights and privileges as detailed on the member benefits matrix. They may not vote or hold office.
- Contributing - Individuals, organizations, institutions, corporations, or foundations which financially support the goals and purposes of the Association. Rights and privileges of the Individual Contributor shall be the same as those for Associate membership, unless the individual or designee qualifies for Professional membership status.
- Affiliate - Organizations and educational institutions that wish to support the goals and objectives of the Association. Rights and privileges of the Individual Designee of an Affiliate member shall be the same as those for Associate membership unless the individual qualifies for Professional membership status.

For more information or to join the American Art Therapy Association, contact:

National Office
American Art Therapy Association
4875 Eisenhower Avenue, Suite 240
Alexandria VA 22304
888-290-0878
703-548-5860
703-783-8468 (FAX)

American Association of Sexuality Educators, Counselors and Therapists

The American Association of Sexuality Educators, Counselors and Therapists (AASECT) is a not-for-profit, interdisciplinary professional organization. In addition to sexuality educators, sexuality counselors and sex therapists, AASECT members include physicians, nurses, social workers, psychologists, allied health professionals, clergy members, lawyers, sociologists, marriage and family counselors and therapists, family planning specialists and researchers, as well as students in relevant professional disciplines. These individuals share an interest in promoting understanding of human sexuality and healthy sexual behavior.

Membership Types:
- Certified Professional Members are those whose membership is

in good standing and who are currently certified with AASECT. These Members are eligible to vote in elections, to hold positions as Officers, as Directors, or as Chairs of Committees, and to serve on all Committees and other functional bodies.

- Professional Members are those whose academic or professional credentials make them eligible to pursue AASECT certification, but who, for whatever reason, are not yet certified by AASECT. These Members are eligible to vote in elections and to serve on all Committees and other functional bodies, but not to hold positions as Officers (with the exception of the position of Treasurer), as Directors, or as Chairs of Committees (with the exception of the Finance Committee). In extraordinary circumstances, the Board of Directors may determine that, in a particular instance and for a specified reason, an exception needs to be made to the requirement that Directors and Chairs of Standing Committees must be Certified Professional Members, and a Professional Member may then hold such a position.

- Supporting Members are those who support the AASECT Mission and Vision of sexual health, but who are not eligible for Professional Membership. These Members are eligible to serve on all Committees and other functional bodies, and to vote within these structures. Supporting Members are also entitled to vote for their Regional Representative on the Membership Services Steering Committee, and for the Chair of the Membership Services Steering Committee, who shall serve on the Board of Directors. Supporting Members shall not be eligible to hold positions as Officers (with the exception of the position of Treasurer), as Directors, or as Chairs of Committees (with the exception of the Finance Committee), nor vote in general elections.

- Student Members are those who support the AASECT mission and vision and are currently enrolled in undergraduate or graduate training at a recognized and accredited educational institution, with a view to becoming eligible for Professional Membership. Annual documentation of student status is required in order to remain in this category of membership. These Members are eligible to serve on all Committees and other functional bodies, and to vote within these structures. Student Members are also entitled to vote for their Regional Representative on the Membership Services Steering Committee, and for the Chair of the Membership Services Steering Committee, who shall serve on the Board of Directors.

Student Members shall not be eligible to hold positions as Officers (with the exception of the position of Treasurer), as Directors, or as Chairs of Committees (with the exception of the Finance Committee), nor vote in general elections.

- Distinguished Honorary Members are those individuals who are recognized by the Board of Directors as having made and outstanding contribution to the field of sexual health and/or to the goals and organization of AASECT. Distinguished Honorary Members will be so elected by the Board of Directors for a specified and time limited duration and shall have such opportunities to vote and serve as the Board of Directors may decide their specific recognition entails.
- Institutional Members are those Professional or Supporting Members who are employed by, or otherwise associated with, a public agency, educational institution, or a professional corporation, that has assumed the responsibility of the dues payment to AASECT. The Board of Directors shall entitle such institutions to nominate three Members to represent the institution within AASECT. Institutional Members have voting rights in accordance with their equivalent status as Professional or Supporting Members.
- Retired Professionals who have reached a retirement of at least 60 years, practice less than full time and/or have greatly reduced their professional income. These Members are eligible to vote in elections and to hold positions on Committees, as Directors or as Officers, according to their prior status as Certified Professional Members or as Professional Members.

For more information on the American Association of Sexuality Educators, Counselors and Therapists (AASECT) or to join, contact:

AASECT
444 I Street, NW, Suite 700
Washington DC 20005
Telephone (202) 449-1099
Fax (202) 216-9646
info@aasect.org
http://www.aasect.org

American Counseling Association

The American Counseling Association (ACA) is a not-for-profit, professional and educational organization that is dedicated to the growth and enhancement of the counseling profession. ACA is the world's largest association exclusively representing professional counselors in various practice settings.

Membership levels:
- ACA Agency Counselor – For ACA members working in an agency
- ACA Private Practice Counselor - For ACA members in private practice
- ACA Student Member – For ACA members who are currently enrolled in a counseling program
- Counselor Educator – For ACA members currently involved in a teaching program related to the counseling profession

For more information about membership, contact:
American Counseling Association
5999 Stevenson Ave.
Alexandria, VA 22304
ACA Fax Number: (703) 823-0252
ACA Toll-Free Numbers: ACA: (800) 347-6647
FAX: (800) 473-2329

For questions regarding membership and address updates, contact Member Services at membership@counseling.org or ext. 222.

American Dance Therapy Association

The American Dance Therapy Association (ADTA), founded in 1966, is a professional organization dedicated to the profession of dance/movement therapy. Dance/movement therapy (DMT) uses movement to further the emotional, cognitive, physical and social integration of the individual. Through movement, DMT can help individuals with a wide range of psychological disorders achieve greater self-expression.

Membership levels:
- Associate Member - Open to - Allied Health Professionals, Creative Arts Therapy Practitioners, Dancers, Educators, Somatic Practitioners, Others
- Associate Member - Open to - Allied Professionals, Creative Arts Practitioners, Dancers, Educators, Somatic Practitioners, Others
- Institutional Member - Open to institutions, schools, organizations, foundations, and supporters contributing annually to the Association. An institutional member has no voting privileges.
- Professional Member - Open to those who have been prepared through graduate dance/movement therapy training or its equivalent. Full voting privileges, may hold office, or serve as a committee chairperson.
- Professional Member - International - Open to those who have

been prepared through graduate dance/movement therapy training or its equivalent. Full voting privileges, may hold office, or serve as a committee chairperson.
- Retired Member - Open to individuals 62 years of age or older, or medically disabled individuals who have been granted Retired Member status.
- Retired Member: International - Open to individuals 62 years of age or older, or medically disabled individuals who have been granted Retired Member status.
- Student Member - Open to all students verified by a student ID card or letter from BC-DMT instructor or supervisor. Limited voting privileges.
- Student Member: High School - Open to all students verified by a student ID card or letter from BC-DMT instructor or supervisor.
- Student Member: International - Open to all students verified by a student ID card or letter from BC-DMT instructor or supervisor.

For more information on membership, or to join, contact:
American Dance Therapy Association
0632 Little Patuxent Parkway
Suite 108
Columbia MD 21044
PHONE: 410-997-4040
FAX: 410-997-4048
Or visit http://www.adta.org

American Music Therapy Association

The American Music Therapy Association (AMTA)'s purpose is the progressive development of the therapeutic use of music in rehabilitation, special education, and community settings. Predecessors, unified in 1998, included the National Association for Music Therapy founded in 1950 and the American Association for Music Therapy founded in 1971. AMTA is committed to the advancement of education, training, professional standards, credentials, and research in support of the music therapy profession.

AMTA Membership levels:
- Professional - Open to music therapists and other professional interested in music therapy. Such membership will provide the privilege of participation in the activities of the Association, both on national and regional levels, including but not limited to the right to vote, to hold office, to receive the Journal of

Music Therapy, Music Therapy Perspectives, and other selected publications of the Association.

- Associate - Open to others, not including music therapists, who support the Association. Associate membership will provide the privilege of participation in the activities of the Association, both on the national and regional levels, and the right to receive the Journal of Music Therapy, Music Therapy Perspectives, and other selected national and regional publications of the Association but does not include the right to vote or hold office.
- Student/Graduate Student - Open to students who are declared music therapy majors enrolled in AMTA-approved schools, or other interested students. Student membership will provide the privilege of participation in the activities of the Association, both on the national and regional levels, and the right to receive the Journal of Music Therapy, Music Therapy Perspectives, and other selected national and regional publications of the Association. Student membership does not include the right to vote or to hold office at the national level. Such rights at the regional level will be as specified by the regional Bylaws.
- Retired - Open to Professional members of AMTA who have reached the age of 65. Rights and privileges will be the same as those for Professional membership. Eligible members must submit a request in writing for transfer to retired status.
- Inactive - Inactive music therapist membership is open to professional music therapists who are not currently practicing music therapy. Music therapists seeking inactive membership must complete an application available from the National Office. Inactive membership will provide the privileges of participation in the activities of the Association and the right to receive selected publications of the Association, but does not include the right to vote or to hold office. To be eligible for Inactive membership, one must: have held active Professional Membership status in AMTA for at least two consecutive years prior to application for inactive status; intend to return to active membership status; not be involved in any professional activity or not working full-time currently due to illness, emergency, childbirth and child rearing, family obligations, etc.; submit an application for inactive status to the AMTA national office.
- Affiliate and Educational Affiliate - Affiliate organization membership will be open to any organization interested in supporting the aims, objectives, and purposes of the

Association. Rights and privileges for the designate of an organization will be the same as those for Associate membership, unless that member qualifies for Professional membership status. The Educational Affiliate designation is for Affiliate members that offer AMTA-approved degree programs in music therapy. Special additional benefits are available to Affiliate and Educational Affiliate members for conference exhibiting and advertising. Please see the member benefits link for more information.

- Patron - Patron membership will be open to individuals, organizations, institutions, business firms, or foundations contributing substantial sums to the Association. Patron membership may be assigned to one person designated by the organization, institution, firm or foundation from which the funds are received. For each contributing year, the Association will confer upon that person the rights and privileges of the type of membership for which the designate would qualify. There are three levels of Patron membership: Patron, Crescendo Patron and Virtuoso Patron. Each level provides special additional benefits depending on the level of membership chosen. Please see the member benefits link for more information.
- Honorary Life - Honorary Life membership may be conferred upon any person in recognition of distinguished service in the field of music therapy. Such election will be made by the Board of Directors. Honorary Life members who qualify for Professional membership will have all the rights and privileges of such membership without the payment of annual dues. Honorary Life membership will be conferred upon a maximum of two persons in any single fiscal year.

For more information about membership or to join, contact:
American Music Therapy Association
8455 Colesville Road, Suite 1000,
Silver Spring MD 20910
Phone: 301.589.3300
Fax: 301.589.5175
Or visit http://www.musictherapy.org

American Psychological Association (APA)

The American Psychological Association (APA) is the national professional organization for psychologists. The APA offers several levels of membership:

- Full Member - Open to people with a doctoral degree in

psychology or a related field from a regionally accredited graduate or professional school (or a school that achieved such accreditation within 5 years of the doctoral degree); or to people with a doctoral degree in psychology or a related field from a foreign institution with equivalency in the United States
- APA Associate Membership - Open to people with a master's degree in psychology or a related field from a regionally accredited institution or a foreign institution with equivalency in the United States; or to people who have completed two years of graduate study in psychology or a related field at a regionally accredited institution or a foreign institution with equivalency in the United States
- APA International Affiliate - Open to psychologists who live outside the United States and Canada
- APA High School Student Affiliate - Open to students who are enrolled as a high school student and interested in a career in psychology or those who want to learn what such a career is all about
- APA Undergraduate or Graduate Student Affiliate - Open to college and university students who are enrolled as an undergraduate or graduate student in an institution of higher learning and who are taking courses in psychology
- APA High School Teacher Affiliate - Open to teachers who teach psychology classes at a high school
- APA Community College Teacher Affiliate - Open to college professors who teach psychology classes at a community college

For more information about membership, write to:
American Psychological Association
750 First St. NE, Washington, DC 20002-4242
Telephone: (800) 374-2721
(202) 336-5500
TDD/TTY: (202) 336-6123
http://www.apa.org

Association for Play Therapy

The Association for Play Therapy (APT) promotes the value of play, play therapy, and credentialed play therapists by advancing the psychosocial development and mental health of all people and sponsoring and supporting those programs, services, and related activities that promote the:
- Public understanding and appreciation of play and play therapy
- Effective practice of play therapy through research, education and training, and support

- Recognition, incorporation, and preservation of diversity in play and play therapy
- Development and maintenance of a strong professional organization that satisfies this mission

The term of membership is for 12 months and renewable in the applicable anniversary month. There are three categories of membership:

- Professional - individual mental health professional within the US
- International - individual mental health professional outside of the US
- Affiliate - individual full-time graduate student or other non-mental health professional

For more information on the Association for Play Therapy, visit http://www.a4pt.org or contact:

Association for Play Therapy, Inc.
3198 Willow Avenue
Suite 110
Clovis CA 93612
Telephone: 559·294·2128
Fax: 559·294·2129
E·mail: info@a4pt.org
http://www.a4pt.org

National Association of Alcohol and Drug Abuse Counselors (NAADAC)

The National Association of Alcohol and Drug Abuse Counselors (NAADAC) is the national professional organization for addiction and substance abuse specialists. NAADAC offers several levels of membership:

- Professional - Open to all individuals who are addiction and/or substance abuse professionals. In some states this is a separate certification and/or licensure. If in doubt, check with your local licensure board.
- Associate - An associate is a person who is working towards certification and/or licensure as an addiction specialist, but who has not yet attained that credential. Associate membership is also available for people who are not addiction specialists, counselors, therapists, psychiatrists, or other behavioral specialists; e.g. probation officers, nurses, etc.
- Student - Open to any students who are enrolled in a program that could lead to licensure and/or certification as an addiction specialist. Students in a full or part-time internship may also be eligible for student membership.

For more information on membership, contact:

National Association of Alcohol and Drug Abuse Counselors (NAADAC)
1001 N. Fairfax St. Suite 201
Alexandria VA 22314
Telephone (703) 741-7686 or (800) 548-0497
Fax (703) 741-7698 or (800) 377-1136
Email naadac@naadac.org

National Association of Social Workers (NASW)

The National Association of Social Workers (NASW) is the largest membership organization of professional social workers in the world, with 140,000 members. NASW works to enhance the professional growth and development of its members, to create and maintain professional standards, and to advance sound social policies.

The National Association of Social Workers (NASW) offers the following levels of membership:

- Regular Full Member - Open to anyone with a Bachelor of Social Work (BSW), Master of Social Work (MSW) or PhD in social work from a school accredited by the Council on Social Work Education (CSWE)
- Student Member - Open to anyone currently enrolled in a social work program accredited by the Council on Social Work Education (CSWE)
- Associate Member - Open to any professional who has an interest in the social work profession

For more information on membership, contact:
National Association of Social Workers
750 First Street, NE
Suite 700
Washington, DC 20002-4241
membership@naswdc.org
Telephone (800) 742-4089

North American Drama Therapy Association

Drama Therapy is an active, experiential approach to facilitating change. Through storytelling, projective play, purposeful improvisation, and performance, participants are invited to rehearse desired behaviors, practice being in relationship, expand and find flexibility between life roles, and perform the change they wish to be and see in the world.

The North American Drama Therapy Association (NADTA) was incorporated in 1979 to establish and uphold rigorous standards of professional competence for drama therapists. The organization maintains requirements that must be met to qualify as a registered drama therapist

(RDT). NADTA promotes drama therapy through information and advocacy.

The North American Drama Therapy Association (NADTA) offers the following Membership Categories:
- Member - Graduates of theatre/drama programs or drama therapists who are using drama for educational and therapeutic purposes.
- Allied Professional - Individuals in other disciplines who are interested in the therapeutic uses of drama/theatre.
- Member 65+ - Members 65 or older. Proof of status is required (copy of driver's license or equivalent).
- Student - Proof of current student status is required.
- Organization/School - Schools, theatres, and other organizations that use drama for educational and therapeutic purposes.

The North American Drama Therapy Association (NADTA) offers the following Registry Categories:
- Professional Registered Drama Therapist (RDT) - Registered drama therapists who have successfully completed the RDT application process and may use the initials RDT; have a Masters degree in drama therapy, theatre, or behavioral science; drama/theatre training; supervised clinical training; and extensive work experience in the field of drama therapy.
- Professional Registered Drama Therapist/Board Certified Teacher (RDT/BCT) - Individuals who have been RDT's for at least five years and successfully completed the application process to be Board Certified as a Teacher/Trainer/Mentor (BCT).

For more information on membership or to join the North American Drama Therapy Association (NADTA), contact:
North American Drama Therapy Association
44365 Premier Plaza, Suite 220
Ashburn, VA 20147
(888) 416-7167
(703) 738-7065
office@nadt.org
http://www.nadt.org

Life Coaching Organizations

A recent trend in America and other countries has been the growth of the 'Life Coaching' industry. Life Coaching began as career and business counseling, but as it has grown it has moved from counseling people on careers to counseling them about life, family, and relationship matters. Life

Coaching is not regulated in most places in the United States. This means that you don't have to have a license or even a certification in order to call yourself a Life Coach. While many Life Coaches are also licensed therapists or counselors, the vast majority of them are not. Many have only completed a short online training program, while still more have completed no training at all before setting up shop.

In most jurisdictions, Life Coaches are not legally allowed to engage in counseling or therapy, since most have little or no training in that area. They are only allowed to 'coach' people. The problem here should be obvious: Where is the line between coaching and counseling? Where is the line between coaching and therapy? Sometimes this can be a difficult line to draw. I've had more than my share of clients who'd been to a Life Coach and received some pretty damaging information about what to do with their lives. Since there is little or no legal accountability for Life Coaches, they are free to give advice with few repercussions.

The International Coach Federation (ICF) claims to be the largest coaching organization in the world. ICF defines coaching as, *"partnering with clients in a thought-provoking and creative process that inspires them to maximize their personal and professional potential. Professional coaches provide an ongoing partnership designed to help clients produce fulfilling results in their personal and professional lives. Coaches help people improve their performances and enhance the quality of their lives. Coaches are trained to listen, to observe and to customize their approach to individual client needs. They seek to elicit solutions and strategies from the client; they believe the client is naturally creative and resourceful. The coach's job is to provide support to enhance the skills, resources and creativity that the client already has."*

As you can see, this definition sounds very close to what counselors and therapists do, but without the oversight of a state licensing board or accountability to any legal entity.

The bottom line on Life Coaching is that unless the Life Coach has specific training in business, finance, or other areas of career development, Life Coaches can't do anything a licensed therapist or counselor couldn't do. Not only that, but Life Coaches are not responsible for answering to any legal authority or licensure board.

Given the average fees that Life Coaches charge for their services, counselors and therapists can usually provide better services less expensively. This is especially true if the therapist or counselor accepts insurance, since Life Coaches aren't covered by insurance.

If you are planning to start a private practice, be aware that Life Coaching is here to stay. It is largely unregulated, and will not be going away in the foreseeable future. As you plan to start your private practice, you may wish to think about how you will work with Life Coaches, as some of your clients will also be clients of Life Coaches.

7 Advertising

When advertising, the main thing to be aware of is that you take care that your advertisements fall within the boundaries of your ethical code. You don't want to misrepresent your skills or your training, but at the same time you want to present yourself in the most positive way possible. It's good to familiarize yourself with your ethical code before composing any advertising copy or before hiring anybody to do it for you. If you are a member of more than one professional organization, you will need to be aware of what each organization's ethical code says about advertising. The ethical code of the American Association of Marriage and Family Therapists (AAMFT) pertaining to advertising will be reviewed and explained below. If your licensure is with another professional organization, review what that organization's ethical code says about advertising in your profession.

The AAMFT says the following about the Ethics of Advertising:

AAMFT Code of Ethics Principle VIII - Advertising
Marriage and family therapists engage in appropriate informational activities, including those that enable the public, referral sources, or others to choose professional services on an informed basis.

8.1 Accurate Professional Representation
Marriage and family therapists accurately represent their competencies, education, training, and experience relevant to their practice of marriage and family therapy.

This means that you cannot claim to have training you do not possess. While this may seem straightforward at first, as with most things pertaining to ethics, it can get a little confusing. Let's look at something as seemingly innocuous as having a doctorate. If you have a doctoral degree in psychology, or family therapy, or some area of counseling or behavioral health, advertising yourself as 'Dr. John Smith' is pretty straightforward. But suppose you have a Masters in some area of behavioral health, and a doctorate in another field. For example, if you have a Masters in Marriage and Family Therapy, and a doctorate in American Literature, it could be argued that if you refer to yourself on your business cards and promotional materials as 'Dr. Jane Doe,' you are misrepresenting your skills and experience. The reason for this is that your doctorate is not in Marriage and Family Therapy, or in any other area of behavioral health. American Literature has little or nothing to do with counseling and therapy. So if you're listed as 'Dr. Jane Doe' without specifically stating that your doctorate is in American Literature, people may automatically assume that your doctorate is in a field related to behavioral health.

That example might seem fairly straightforward, but in other areas there are more shades of grey. Suppose, for instance, that you have a Doctor of Ministry or a Doctor of Divinity degree. Some such doctoral programs offer classes in counseling and therapy from a spiritual perspective, while others do not. Is it ethical in such a case to list yourself as a 'doctor'? What about a doctoral degree in psychology education? While such a degree may focus on certain aspects of behavioral health, is it really a degree that focuses on education specifically relating to counseling and therapy?

Another issue regarding education is exactly what the ethical code means by 'training' and 'education.' All good behavioral health programs include at least some training in, for example, anger management. Yet there are also certifications and training that are geared specifically towards dealing with people who have anger management issues. If you haven't taken any continuing education courses specific to anger management, but have had some training in this area in your graduate degree program, can you advertise yourself as an 'Anger Management Specialist?'

To be on the safe side when these questions and others like them arise, you can always check with your local licensure board and your local professional organization. Professional organizations have specialists on staff to answer such questions. It may also help to seek training in the ethics of advertising.

8.2 Promotional Materials

Marriage and family therapists ensure that advertisements and publications in any media (such as directories, announcements, business cards, newspapers, radio, television, Internet, and facsimiles) convey information that is necessary for the public to make an appropriate selection of professional services and consistent with applicable law.

This section means that in addition to making sure that information in your ads is accurate, you should also not commit any 'sins of omission' by failing to include important information in your ads. For example, if your office isn't handicapped accessible, you might want to include that in your promotional materials. If you don't accept insurance, that might be an important thing to include as well. A good rule of thumb is to view your advertising through the eyes of a potential client with little or no experience in evaluating therapists. If such a person read your ad, would they have all the information they need to make an informed decision on whether or not to engage your services?

Another aspect of this section is that you are responsible for any errors in your advertising, even if it was the publisher's fault and not your own. If any erroneous information is accidentally printed, it is your responsibility to print a correction or a retraction as soon as possible. A common error here is that the general public tends to assume that all therapists are doctors. So when your ad is in the copy department, copy writers like to insert 'Dr.' before your name, even if you are a Masters level clinician. Proofread any ads before they're printed, and proofread them again after they've been published. Post retractions and corrections as needed.

8.3 Professional Affiliations

Marriage and family therapists do not use names that could mislead the public concerning the identity, responsibility, source, and status of those practicing under that name, and do not hold themselves out as being partners or associates of a firm if they are not.

8.4 Professional Identification
Marriage and family therapists do not use any professional identification (such as a business card, office sign, letterhead, Internet, or telephone or association directory listing) if it includes a statement or claim that is false, fraudulent, misleading, or deceptive.

These are pretty straightforward and self-explanatory, but there are some areas to watch out for that could potentially land you in ethical hot water.

Section 8.3 is about accurately representing yourself in relation to professional affiliation. The obvious point here is that Marriage and Family Therapists do not misrepresent their licensure and training; however, there are also less obvious aspects of this section. Suppose you go into practice with a pre-existing entity whose specialization is addiction treatment. Further suppose you have little or no training in addiction treatment. Is it accurate representation of your skills to call yourself an associate of this organization?

If you are a member of any group practice, including a partnership, that advertises your services, you are also personally liable for anything the organization advertises about their skills and services. So if there are any misrepresentations in their advertising, you can be held personally liable for those representations, just by being a member of the organization. It is your duty to examine all advertising materials for any organization with which you are associated in order to determine that there are no misrepresentations, omissions, or misleading copy.

Section 8.4 is about identity and avoiding misrepresentation. This also seems like a no-brainer, but there is room for confusion even here. Consider the possibility of earning your license under your maiden name, then getting married. Will clients be able to clearly identify who you are, and distinguish between the two? Another possible gray area: Suppose you are in a PhD program, and you have finished everything but your doctoral dissertation. Ethically, you cannot call yourself 'doctor' on your business materials until you've completed all of the requirements for your doctorate, including the dissertation. You could theoretically list yourself as 'ABD,' which stands for 'all but dissertation,' but since the general public doesn't usually know what 'ABD' stands for, this could potentially be construed as misrepresentation or at least, lack of clarity in representing yourself.

Starting a Family Therapy Business

8.5 Educational Credentials
In representing their educational qualifications, marriage and family therapists list and claim as evidence only those earned degrees: (a) from institutions accredited by regional accreditation sources; (b) from institutions recognized by states or provinces that license or certify marriage and family therapists; or (c) from equivalent foreign institutions.

In an age of online degrees, it's very easy to get into a quagmire of accreditation rules and regulations. While there are online programs that are accredited by regional accreditation sources, there are also online programs that are not accredited by any source. According to Section 8.5, if your degree and/or licensure are not from an accredited and recognized institution, then you are ethically forbidden from calling yourself a Marriage and Family Therapist.

People usually run into problems in this area with seminary degrees. If you are a Doctor of Ministry or a Doctor of Divinity, check with your local licensure board to make sure your degree is from a recognized program and that listing yourself as a doctor on your promotional materials would not violate any ethical codes or state laws in your region.

8.6 Correction of Misinformation
Marriage and family therapists correct, wherever possible, false, misleading, or inaccurate information and representations made by others concerning the therapist's qualifications, services, or products.

This section includes simple mistakes as well as deliberate errors of omission and misrepresentation. If a third party makes a mistake in advertising your credentials and experience, your services, or your products, you have an ethical obligation to correct such misrepresentations as quickly as possible. This is true whether the mistake or the misrepresentation was your fault or not. Probably the most common error in this department occurs during newspaper, television or radio interviews when the interviewer refers to a Masters level clinician as 'doctor.' This is also common with patients, who tend to think that all therapists are doctors. It can sometimes become tedious to constantly correct a patient who insists on calling you 'doctor,' but ethically you are obliged to do so every time they make the error. It may help to explain to them why it is inappropriate to use the title with you if you have not earned a doctorate related to behavioral health.

8.7 Employee or Supervisee Qualifications
Marriage and family therapists make certain that the qualifications of their employees

or supervisees are represented in a manner that is not false, misleading, or deceptive.

Obviously this would only be an issue if you have any employees or supervisees. The thing to watch for here is what constitutes 'employee' or 'supervisee.' If someone works in your office as a contractor or consultant, then legally they are deemed to be an employee of yours, and therefore subject to the ethical code. If they misrepresent themselves or their skills while in your employ, you are ethically obligated to correct such errors, and to make sure that it doesn't happen again. You can be held liable for any misrepresentation or omission committed by any employees in your service.

8.8 Specialization
Marriage and family therapists do not represent themselves as providing specialized services unless they have the appropriate education, training, or supervised experience.

This is yet another section that seems to be straightforward at first glance, but it has the potential to cause problems if not properly understood. The meaning of this section, like others, is vague and open to interpretation. What exactly constitutes *appropriate* education, training, or supervised experience? Would a one-hour online course in Play Therapy be sufficient education and training to advertise yourself as a 'Play Therapy Specialist'? If you had a course in Art Therapy during your graduate or undergraduate degree program, could you legally call yourself an Art Therapist, since there is an entire separate certification process for Art Therapy? If you took a one-day training in Mindfulness, could you then call yourself an expert in Mindfulness-Based Cognitive Therapy? Since there is an entire program and certification process for Mindfulness-Based Cognitive Therapy, is it a misrepresentation to cite this as a specialty if you haven't been through that particular certification process?

Training and education can get confusing in a hurry, especially when listing yourself as a specialist. When in doubt, it's better to check with your local licensure board than it is to open yourself up to a potential lawsuit.

Types of Advertising

There are many types of advertising you might choose for your private practice. There are advantages and disadvantages to each method, and the next sections will look at some of those. No form of advertising is entirely foolproof. It will take some trial and error to determine which methods work best for you, and results vary from region to region based on the buying habits of local consumers.

The types of advertising we will be examining will be radio, television, newspapers, magazines, newsletters, online advertising, direct mailing campaigns, business cards, brochures and flyers, t-shirts and specialty items.

We'll also discuss some ways to get free advertising and free publicity by hosting your own events, making public speeches and presentations, and other news events.

Radio

Radio was once a powerhouse of advertising, but in these days of multimedia and on-demand music programming, this medium is a shadow of its former self. Still, there are some places and situations where radio might be a good choice.

The main advantage of radio is that it is wide-reaching. Anyone with a receiver within the station's broadcast range can pick up the signal for free, and potentially hear your advertisement. In some cases, radio will even allow you to target specific demographics. Talk radio AM stations tend to cater to older populations, pop music stations are geared towards a younger audience, and public radio tends to have affluent middle class listeners.

In web-based radio, you can get even more specific in targeting a demographic, as many web radio stations collect demographic data on their listeners specifically for this purpose. The potential disadvantage with web-based radio is that its audience is worldwide rather than local, so a large percentage of your listeners might not live within driving distance of your private practice. Some internet radio stations allow you to specifically target listeners in your area, for a price, so this might not always be a disadvantage.

One of the major disadvantages of radio is that it is expensive for the amount of return on investment. Even though you can target a demographic within certain parameters with radio advertising, you're still reaching a lot of people who aren't interested. When's the last time you heard a radio ad for a therapist? For most private practice therapy offices, the investment just isn't worth the return.

Television

An advantage of television is that it usually reaches an even wider audience than radio. Most people who listen to radio do so while driving to and from work. Their minds are on traffic and not on radio ads. People watch television in their own homes, so they're usually more attentive, assuming they didn't get up during the commercials to make a sandwich or go to the bathroom.

Another advantage of television is that you can target demographics based on the type of shows they're likely to watch. If your key demographic is teenagers and adolescents, you're going to want your commercials to run during different shows than you would if your key demographic is retired married couples.

If you have personal charisma you can use it to your advantage in a television spot. As a therapist or counselor, your product is yourself. The more you can sell yourself, the more customers you will have. A thirty second or one minute television spot offers potential clients a free sample of your product.

One of the disadvantages of television is that it is even more expensive than radio, with the same limited return on investment. You're putting out a lot of cash flow for a limited return. Unless you're Dr. Phil, don't expect a lot of new clients from a television spot.

Another potential disadvantage of television advertising is 'stalker syndrome.' For some reason, people who appear on television seem to attract more celebrity stalkers than those who appear on radio or in newspaper ads. This is probably due to the fact that television is a visual medium, and it's easier to pick out faces that have been on television than it is to pick out voices from the radio. The real danger of being stalked is minimal, so don't be overly alarmed at this potential disadvantage. Such cases are very rare, but they do exist.

Another disadvantage of television advertising is that it may take a long time to work. The longer it takes to bring paying customers to your door, the more money you're paying out with limited returns. As already mentioned, most people are making sandwiches or taking bathroom breaks during the commercials, so unless your audience is actually in front of the television when your commercial airs, it goes without saying that they're not going to see it.

Yellow Pages & Other Telephone Directories

About the only advantage of advertising in a printed telephone directory is that you get to see your name in print. In this era of personal computing and smart phones, the only people who look up numbers in a telephone directory are people who can't afford a personal computer or a smart phone. Unless you accept Medicaid or Medicare, such people will rarely be able to afford your services. You already get a standard listing for free if your number is listed publicly. Don't spend extra on advertising that very few people will see. Think about it: When is the last time you used a telephone directory to find a business or service?

Newspapers

One of the primary advantages of newspaper advertising is that it is less expensive than radio or television. There is also the 'cast off' effect with newspapers: Because people tend to pass newspapers on to other people, more than one person might read the same newspaper.

Another advantage of newspaper advertising is that because of the lower cost, you can run ads over a longer period of time, increasing the likelihood of people reading your ad.

Even with the lower cost, there is the issue of the relevance of newspapers in an electronic age. When's the last time you read a newspaper? Fewer people subscribe to newspapers these days, preferring to get their news and information from online sources. If your advertisement doesn't get read, you've wasted your money. Unless the ad is big enough to catch the reader's attention, research shows that most people ignore it. The larger the ad, the better the chances are of it being noticed. But of course larger ads are more expensive.

Another disadvantage of newspaper advertising is that it is hard to target a specific demographic unless it's a specialty newspaper. You can increase your chances of getting referrals by advertising in specific sections. For example, if you specialize in marriage counseling, you could run ads in your local paper's wedding section. If you do grief counseling, you could request to have your ad placed near the obituaries. If you work with children, check to see if your newspaper has a section that caters to parents or children.

Overall, given the decline of newspaper readership, newspaper ads can take a long time to show any return on investment.

Magazines

Many magazines operate in the realm of niche markets. There's pretty much a magazine for every interest and hobby. Because of this niche marketing, it's easier to target a specific demographic with newspaper advertising. If you have a specialty you can look for magazines that match up with your special skills, just as you can target a particular demographic by advertising in certain sections of the newspaper. Try to stay away from advertising in psychology journals and counseling magazines. With such ads you tend to be a small fish in a very big pond, since most other therapists are running ads in those magazines.

Magazines tend to have even more 'cast off' value than newspapers, as magazines tend to have longer shelf life. Since most are published monthly or even bi-monthly, many people tend to hold on to them longer. Also, since the content tends to be more in-depth than that of the average newspaper, people may save them for a longer period of time. If you've ever picked up an ancient magazine in your doctor's office, you already know that sometimes these magazines, and therefore your advertisement, will be around for awhile.

Some magazines are regional or even local in nature, allowing for even more select targeting of demographics. If your city or town publishes a magazine for locals, this would probably be your best bet for magazine ads.

One potential disadvantage of magazine advertising is that magazines tend to be more expensive than newspapers, so people may not buy them as often. Another disadvantage is that since magazines are usually published less frequently than newspapers, you don't get as much market saturation.

Yet another disadvantage of magazines is that your ad has to be read in order to be effective. How often do people actually pay attention to magazine ads unless they're actually looking for something specific?

Newsletters

Newsletters, by their very nature, target certain demographics. Newsletters tend to be even more specialized in nature than magazines. Because of this, you have a better chance of getting your ad in front of the right people. Another advantage of newsletters is that you can create your own, and have visitors to your website elect to subscribe to it. Because your newsletter goes out in email, the only costs involved are your monthly Internet bill and the time and effort required to design and compose it. If you choose to advertise in a pre-existing printed newsletter, the ads are usually less expensive than most other forms of print media.

Since newsletters usually only come out on a monthly basis, there is not as much saturation as you might get with a daily or weekly newspaper ad. This is made up for to some degree by the cast off effect where people pass newsletters on to friends, family and co-workers.

Due to the narrow nature of the audience of most newsletters, you might not reach your specific demographics if you have more than one specialty. If you specialize, for instance, in marital counseling and play therapy, advertising in a newsletter that only caters to parents and children may get you referrals for play therapy, but not as many for marital counseling.

Another disadvantage of newsletters is that they tend to have less shelf life than magazines. This is balanced by the fact that they do have a bit more shelf life than the average newspaper.

Direct Mailing

Direct mailing involves sending letters, postcards, brochures and other mailings directly to a person's or a business's mailbox. Direct mail campaigns are probably the best campaigns for precision targeting of specific demographics. With direct mailing, it's easier to target a specific demographic because you're choosing who to send your mailings to, so you have all the control.

If you have an address book full of contacts, you can send them announcements about events at your private practice. If your address book is a little thin on potential referrals, you can also buy lists of addresses from direct mail marketing companies. Although many of these companies allow you to custom-design your purchased mailing lists based on characteristics of your target demographic, these companies usually don't update their listings very frequently, so there's the potential of getting a lot of returned letters if you decide to go this route.

One alternative is that you can 'job it out' to professional mailing services. These companies already have existing mailing lists, and you just pay a fee for them to design, print, and mail out your announcements and advertisements. You can measure how effective such mailings are by including 'code words' in the ad. For example, "Bring this advertisement in and your first session is free!" If the advertisement contains such a code word, you can then analyze which mailing it came from in order to know which mailings are working and which are not.

If you offer things like discounts and free sessions, check first with your local laws and your own ethical code to make sure such offers are legal and ethical.

A major disadvantage of direct mailing is the expense. The more people you intend to reach, the more money you'll have to spend in postage and materials. Another disadvantage is that many people see such mailings as 'junk mail,' and they get tossed in the bin without being read. There is usually about a 1% return on direct mailing. This means that for every 100 mailings, one person responds, and then only a fraction of those who respond actually book an appointment.

Another disadvantage is concerns with confidentiality. If you are mailing to individuals rather than to businesses, some people may be offended at the prospect of receiving mailings from a mental health professional. A final disadvantage is that there are environmental implications to mass mailings. Since the majority of such mailings get tossed into the trash can without being read, the ones that get tossed are wasted paper. Even if environmental concerns don't worry you, there will be potential clients who may be offended that you are sending paper products when email is available.

Business Cards

Business cards are by far the best and cheapest form of advertising. This is especially true when attending conferences and other networking opportunities. It's a good idea to keep some in your pocket or purse at all times so that you can get into the habit of leaving them at restaurants, book stores, seminars, coffee shops, bulletin boards, offices, and anywhere else you go on your daily errands.

Business cards can be printed off on your computer at home, or obtained fairly inexpensively from most commercial printers. They're a convenient size for slipping into wallets, purses, and pockets. Because of this, people tend to hang on to them.

A disadvantage of business cards is that they are still easily tossed aside in spite of their convenient size. They're better used in a one-on-one networking situation, although they can occasionally bring in multiple referrals if pinned to a bulletin board.

If you're leaving multiple business cards on a table somewhere for people to pick up, you may want to engage the services of a professional graphic designer. If your cards don't get noticed, they don't get picked up, and if your graphic design skills are limited, it may be hard to get noticed.

Brochures

Brochures are a bit larger than business cards, and can therefore contain a bit more information about your services, but they are still small enough to fit in a pocket or purse. Because of this convenient size, you can leave them at restaurants, book stores, seminars, coffee shops, on bulletin boards, and virtually anywhere else such materials are left for public distribution.

While brochures are slightly more expensive than business cards, they are still relatively inexpensive when compared with other forms of advertising. The most common variety of brochure is the tri-fold brochure. Most word processing programs even have a template for a tri-fold brochure so you can print them out yourself on your home computer. If you plan to go this route, buy some glossy paper specifically designed for this process. If you print your brochures on standard printer paper, the ink tends to bleed through and the result is a very unprofessional-looking product. Remember that you never get a second chance to make a first impression, and your brochure is the first impression most people will have of your business, so make it a quality, professional job. If you're unsure of your design and composition skills, have your printer or graphic designer create a brochure for you. This can be done relatively inexpensively.

Many of the disadvantages of brochures are the same disadvantages of business cards. They are easily tossed aside and are therefore best used in one-on-one situations where you know the person has at least some interest in your services in the first place.

If you have little or no experience in marketing, you may need professional help in determining what sort of information to include in your brochure. A good rule of thumb is to include the following information in your brochures:

- Who is your target demographic?
- What services do you offer?
- When do you schedule appointments?
- What are your office hours?
- Where are you located?
- How would a person schedule an appointment with you?
- What insurance, EAPs and HMOs do you accept?
- What are your fees (you may not want to include this

information on your brochures; instead, save it for your initial consultation)
- Why should a person choose your services over every other therapist's in town?

Remember that as with business cards, if your brochures don't get noticed, they don't get picked up, so make them noticeable!

Tips for Business Cards & Brochures

Business cards and brochures are a private practice therapist's bread and butter. Carry them with you at all times. Make it a habit to pick them up any time you leave your office. Sleep with them if you have to!

Distribute your business cards and brochures anywhere you can as you go about your day-to-day errands. Take large amounts of both to business conferences, health fairs and trainings for distribution.

If you plan to use a tri-fold brochure as your primary business advertisement, remember that such a brochure can also be used as a mailer. The middle back section of such a brochure can be designed for a place with a return address and a mailing address. The brochure may then be folded to resemble an envelope, and sealed for mailing.

An advantage of printing your own brochures is that you may choose to make several for different occasions. If your specialty is marriage counseling, you might send some out in February for Valentine's Day or in June, when a large number of people are planning their weddings. If your specialty is suicide prevention, you might send some out for Suicide Prevention Month, or during the holiday season when risk of suicide increases. If your specialty is addiction treatment, you might send some out during the holidays in which driving while intoxicated is at increased risk (for example, Labor Day Weekend, Independence Day, or New Year's Day).

With a little imagination and a lot of fine tuning, both business cards and brochures can be turned into a powerful marketing tool that will work to your advantage. With a little trial and error, you'll discover the right combination for your own private practice.

T-Shirts & Specialty Items

Specialty advertising includes items that can be printed with your logo, address, slogan, or other advertising message. Such items include t-shirts, pens, bumper stickers, coffee mugs, water bottles, key chains, or virtually any other gift item that can be printed.

Specialty items have a long shelf life, giving your logo continuing 'brand' exposure. They are also a more personalized reminder of your business. Since they are a gift, people will be more likely to use them, thereby giving you exposure.

While specialty printed items are fairly expensive, they are usually not as expensive as other forms of advertising. If you've ever gotten a free pen or a free t-shirt at an event, you know that people enjoy such promotional items.

A major disadvantage of specialty items such as this is the confidentiality factor. Due to the persisting stigma of behavioral disorders, some people may hesitate to wear a t-shirt with your logo on it because they don't want anybody knowing they're going to a therapist. For this reason, specialty items might be better distributed at doctor's offices and other community health care facilities among the employees, where people are likely to refer to you.

Another disadvantage is that there is usually a fairly long turnaround time for imprinted items of anywhere from two weeks to two months, depending on the type of merchandise and the quantity.

A final disadvantage is that in order for specialty item advertising to work, you need a distribution outlet for the merchandise. This could be turned into an advantage, though. You could run a promotion along the lines of "Come by our office for a free t-shirt!"

Before running such a promotion, make sure your state's laws and ethical codes allow such promotions.

Permission Marketing

If you've ever been to a website and clicked on a newsletter link for the purpose of subscribing, you've given your permission to be included in that website's mailings. Because of this consent, such website offerings are referred to as *permission marketing*.

The advantage of permission marketing is that it greatly increases the chance that your ads and announcements will be seen by people who are interested in your services. The simple fact that they've granted you permission to send them newsletters and advertisements, tells you that they have some interest in your product. I do extensive permission marketing by email when I send out my email newsletter every month.

Facebook, Google, LinkedIn & other Social Media

You may have used social media outlets like Facebook, Google, and LinkedIn, but did you know you can advertise on such sites as well? All of these forms of advertising can be powerful and flexible forms of marketing. If you advertise with any of these media outlets, you are given a wide range of demographic data options so that you can easily target the types of people who you want to see your ads. You can also set your budget for each advertising campaign. Once you reach your target amount, the ads don't show any more, and you no longer get charged for them.

Such advertising usually works on a 'pay per click' basis. What this means is that you create an ad, then you bid on how much you're willing to pay if someone clicks on it. Every time someone clicks on your ad, you pay a fee up to the amount you bid. Once you've reached your target amount for the day, your ad stop showing until the next day.

For example, let's say I bid one dollar per click on my ad, and I set my daily budget at $10. This means that the most I would pay per click on my ad would be $1, and once I'd spent my $10 daily budget paying for clicks, my ad would stop showing for the day. If there are at least ten clicks per day at $1 each, and my daily budget is $10, that means that my daily financial outlay would be at most $10. Of course, if less than ten people per day click on the ad, it would be less. But it would never cost me more than $10 per day, or $300 per month in the average month.

If nobody clicks on my ad, then I pay nothing for that day. But of course, the idea is to get people to click on the ad. Since the amount of text in such ads is usually limited, the idea is to post a link to your website somewhere in the ad so that people who click on it are directed to your website, where you can include as much text and information as you want.

Pay-per-click on social media sites is by far the best 'bang for your buck' in advertising. You can specifically target demographics based on a wide variety of parameters like age, marital status, location, race, and many other categories. If you've ever filled out a survey to join a social media site, you're familiar with the type of demographic data such sites collect. If the site is collecting demographic data, you can probably target your advertising based on that demographic data.

There are, however, some disadvantages to social media advertising. One is that due to the global nature of such ads, it's sometimes hard to target local demographics. If your private practice is located in a specific city, do you target only people living in that city, or do you expand the range to include the surrounding areas? How far would people be willing to drive for your services? I've had regular clients who routinely drove over a hundred miles for their appointment.

Another potential disadvantage to social media advertising is that people using social media are not usually thinking about buying something. This is especially true for therapy services. Studies have shown that advertising on social media sites has a less than 2% return on investment overall. The percentage is even lower for therapy services.

When advertising on social media, you have to have a fairly high budget to get consistent results. The more you're willing to spend, the more likely your ad is to pop up on relevant social media pages. It can be hit-or-miss as to whether the right people get to see your ad. This is even true with specifically targeted demographics. Think about it: If you needed a therapist, would your first thought be to hop on Facebook to look for one?

Insurance Websites

Once you start getting accepted on insurance company panels, you will be given the opportunity to have a profile page on the company's website. Some insurance companies do this automatically, while others only give you a password that grants you access to their profile pages, then leave it up to you to fill in the blanks.

Insurance websites are usually highly optimized for search engines. What this means is that if a person is looking for a mental health provider, a highly optimized site shows up in the top of the search engine results. Realistically speaking, people searching for a behavioral health provider are only likely to search their own insurance company's website. That means that if I have Blue Cross insurance, I'm not going to be looking on CIGNA's website for a provider, even if CIGNA comes up ahead of Blue Cross in a search engine. So having your profile page show up high in the search engine rankings on a particular insurance company's website is only useful if the person doing the searching has that particular brand of insurance.

People generally search for providers in their area, so if you're in an urban area, you're likely to get more referrals from local people. The exception to this is if a person feels some stigma attached to seeing a therapist. In such a case, they might be willing to drive a greater distance to maintain anonymity. I've had people drive two hours for their weekly appointment because of this stigma.

A drawback to having an office in an urban area is that there is likely to be a fairly large number of other providers on the same insurance panels in the same area. Many of the larger urban areas have reached market saturation and are no longer accepting providers in those congested areas. I mention this because simply being accepted on an insurance panel is no guarantee of referrals from that insurance company. The exception to this would be if you offer a service or specialty that is unique and different from all the other providers listed with that insurance company in your geographical region. If that's the case, don't forget to include that information in your provider profile on the insurance company's website!

In addition to offering a unique service, another way to get referrals is to get out and network with your local representatives of that insurance company. Do you work with a psychiatrist who takes the same forms of insurance that you do? If so, that psychiatrist would probably be more likely to refer patients with that insurance to you, because of the smooth transition. The patient will know that you accept her insurance because the psychiatrist knows that you accept her insurance.

A disadvantage of using insurance panel provider profile pages is that the content needs to be constantly updated. A good rule of thumb is to plan to add fresh content at least once a month. Every time you attend a continuing education event, it's a good idea to get into the habit of updating all your provider pages with your new credentials. The more often you do so, the more likely you are to get referrals.

Another disadvantage of insurance websites is that when a potential client searches for providers they not only see your profile page, but also every other provider's page within the same zip code. So unless you have a specialty that the client is interested in, it's difficult to stand out from the crowd. Some insurance panel websites will move your ranking closer to the top the more often you add new content, so the more you're able to do this, the more likely you are to get bumped to the top of the listings.

Professional Organization Websites

If you join a professional organization such as the American Association of Marriage and Family Therapists or the National Association of Social Workers, or another professional organization, you are usually entitled to a free profile page on their website. Such a profile page can be a great way to network with other members of the organization. If, however, you are seeking referrals for patients from such websites, don't set your hopes too high. In all my years as a Marriage and Family Therapist, I've only gotten one referral from the AAMFT website, and that person didn't schedule an appointment.

For laypersons with little or no experience in various different types of counseling and therapy, professional organizations can be a bewildering alphabet soup of credentials. If you've never heard of Marriage and Family Therapy, you're not likely to know that there's a website for the American Association of Marriage and Family Therapists. If you don't know that such a website exists, then you're not going to know that you can search for a therapist on that website. Sadly, many professional organizations don't invest a lot in search engine optimization, so people doing online searches for therapy and counseling are not likely to find a website for your particular professional organization unless they're deliberately looking for it.

This doesn't mean that such profile pages are futile. Professionals often use such websites for networking purposes. If I don't specialize in Play Therapy, for example, and I need a therapist who does, I can always go to the AAMFT website to find a therapist with that credential. I may also go to the Play Therapy Association's website to find someone. Because of this, the chief sources of referral from professional organization websites tend to be from other professionals who are either also members of the same organization, or who frequently use the organization's website as a resource.

Your Own Website

Having your own website is by far the most inexpensive method of advertising. Depending on the bells and whistles you want on your website, most hosting companies charge between $5 and $10 per month to host your website. Once your site is up, anyone in the world with Internet access can view your site.

One caveat with your own website is that if you don't have any experience in designing your website, or if you don't have a friend who can do it for you, such services can be expensive. Website design can range anywhere from several hundred to several thousand dollars, depending on your needs and content. The good news is that with some of the newer content management systems, you don't have to have a lot of programming skills in order to be able to design your own site. If you can use a word processor you can design your own website with content management systems like WordPress and DRUPAL.

If you have your own website, you have total control over the content. Your site can be as big or as small as you want. You may also target key demographics by incorporating different 'landing pages' for different populations. By assigning keywords specific to your target demographic, you are able to attract them to your website. If, for example, you specialize in substance abuse, you might use keywords like, "addiction," "substance abuse," "dependence," "self-medicating," etc. to make sure the right people are able to find your site.

Another way to drive traffic to your site is to provide free information as a customer service. You can do this by placing links and resources on your website, or you might do it by starting a blog through one of the free online blogging services. 'Blog' is short for 'web log,' and it is simply an Internet-based periodic journal or article. Some people choose to blog once a month, while others blog once a week. By adding fresh content to your blog on a regular basis, you keep visitors returning to your site. If you write well, you will attract people to your website to see what you have to say in your next blog entry.

If you don't write well, don't despair. You can achieve a similar effect by periodically searching for new articles and studies related to your topics of interest, and posting links to them on your own site. If you do this, make sure that you have the author's permission first!

A major disadvantage of having your own website is that if they can't find your website, they won't see it. If a potential client has no knowledge of the address to your website, the only way they can find it is through an Internet search. This is done through a variety of search engines. The current most popular search engine is Google. Search Engine Optimization (SEO) is a necessity for making sure that your website scores high in the rankings for searches related to your areas of expertise.

Google Analytics is a free tool that Google provides to help you to optimize your website for search engines. You can do your own SEO if you have the time and the patience to learn this, or you can hire someone to do it for you. The more money you're willing to spend, the better quality SEO service you can hire. A word of caution when hiring a SEO company: As with many things on the Internet, there are a lot of scam artists out there. Check with your local Chamber of Commerce or Better Business Bureau for a reputable company in your area.

If you don't have the expertise to design your own website and manage your own search engine optimization, it can be quite expensive to contract out. My advice would be to do it anyway, since it is the most powerful advertising tool in your arsenal. Be aware that if you intend to design your own website and do your own SEO, that content needs to be constantly updated in order to maintain search engine rankings. The more fresh content you add on a regular basis, the more likely you are to place high in the rankings in most search engines.

If you're doing your own search engine optimization, you should be aware that SEO 'rules' are constantly changing. What works this month might not work next month. If you're planning to do it yourself, expect for optimizing your website to be an ongoing process. You may wish to subscribe to a newsletter or emailing group that specializes in SEO tips and tricks so that you can keep up-to-date. If you plan to hire someone to do this for you, realize that this will be a permanent position. At a minimum you should engage such services at least every six months to make sure your website continues to place in the rankings with the major search engines.

There are many things to consider for inclusion when looking for content on your website. It's a good idea to ask yourself what sort of information you'd be seeking about a therapist if you were a potential client. At a bare minimum you should have the name and address of the practice, contact information, a brief biography and information about your training and credentials, information about your clinical approach and specialties, and information about what types of insurance, EAPs and HMOs you accept, if any. It's probably not a good idea to include fee information on your website unless absolutely necessary. The reason for this is that if your fee is higher than prospective clients are willing to pay, they'll automatically reject you before talking to you. If they have to call you for fee information, you have the opportunity to 'sell' yourself a bit before getting down to negotiating a fee. You will, of course, have to have a fee agreement in your intake paperwork, but unless the laws in your state specifically require you to put fee information on your website, it's probably a good idea to discuss fees over the telephone instead.

Free Advertising

It goes without saying that free advertising is the best type of advertising, and there are plenty of opportunities to get free publicity if you know where to look.

One type of advertising that doesn't cost anything is blogging. If you enjoy writing, creating a blog on one of the free blogging services allows you to create content on a periodic basis that will drive traffic to your website, as discussed in the previous section. Just make sure to include a link to your website when you update your blog.

Another excellent source of free advertising for therapists is health fairs. Most major urban hospitals have at least one health fair per year. While such health fairs usually charge sponsors a fee for having a table at such an event, you might be able to offer your services in exchange for free space instead. I've done free depression and substance abuse screenings at such health fairs in exchange for permission to hand out brochures advertising my services. Such screenings consist of a checklist of diagnostic criteria that attendees at the health fair fill out and score themselves. If they have enough criteria to be a concern, I hand them a brochure and ask them to schedule an appointment for a complete assessment.

If there is no health fair in your area, you might consider sponsoring one yourself. Get together with other health care professionals in your area to see if they might be interested in joining in with you for such an event. Colleges and universities might be a good venue for such events. Ask the Student Activities Director of your local college if they'd be interested in hosting your health fair. Once you've got it organized, you can ask the school to help you promote it. You can also usually get free public service announcements at local media outlets to promote the event (see the section on *Public Service Announcements* below).

If you're lucky enough to have access to a conference room in your office, you might also consider sponsoring a free workshop on your area of expertise. You can either tailor such workshops to the general public or to therapists and counselors who might be interested in learning more. If you don't have access to a conference room, you might be able to sponsor a day-long event and split the costs with other therapists. If you are a member of a church or organization that might let you use their meeting space for free, you have the added advantage of promoting the event on their bulletin boards.

Another good source of free advertising is public speaking engagements. Most nonprofit organizations hold periodic fundraising events, and they are always in need of speakers for such events. Social clubs also frequently need guest speakers, as do schools, colleges, and universities. Churches and civic organizations are especially good sources of speaking opportunities. If you're comfortable speaking in public, there are several websites that match speakers with organizations needing speakers. If asked to present a speech at an event, make sure to carry your business cards and brochures for distribution before, during, and after the event.

Public Service Announcements

Most newspapers, television and radio stations offer public service announcements for free for select organizations. Such free announcements are usually limited to non-profit organizations, but they may also be available for free events sponsored by for-profit organizations as well. If you host a health fair, workshop, or other free event, many of these media outlets are likely to announce it for you for no cost.

Newspaper, Radio and Television Stories

Most local media outlets, especially in smaller towns, are starved for stories. Because of this, if you have any news of human interest, it's always a good idea to contact your local newspapers, radio and television stations to see if they might be interested in covering your event. They might not always say "yes," but if you don't ask, the answer will *always* be "no."

A good time to approach the local media is when you first open your business. Have a ribbon-cutting ceremony and invite all the local reporters. You may also wish to invite key city officials like the Mayor, the Director of the local Mental Health Association, and anyone else you can think of who might be interested in attending your open house ceremony.

Other opportunities for public service announcements include any event sponsored by your private practice. This could be health fairs, workshops, seminars, classes, groups, or any other event that the public might like to know about.

Magazine Articles

If your city or town publishes any local magazines, you might consider approaching them to do a piece on your private practice, or some aspect of it. If you have any writing skills, you might also want to ask them if they'd be interested in having you write a regular column for them. If not, maybe they'd at least be interested in having you write a piece on a subject involving your particular areas of expertise. If they turn you down for now, don't forget to ask them to keep you in mind should any opportunities arise in the near future. Don't forget to keep checking back every few months. There's a lot of turnover in the publishing industry, and tomorrow's editor might not turn you down.

Advertising: The Key is Persistence

It may take quite some time before you determine which particular combination of advertising strategies will work for your particular situation and in your particular area. Don't give up, and don't get discouraged. You will eventually hit upon the winning formula. It may help to keep a journal of what types of advertising seem to bring in the most clients. I have a space on my intake paperwork that asks, "How did you hear about me?"

That question helps me to determine which types of advertising are working, and which are not. It's critical that you track your results in some way or another so that you don't waste your hard-earned money paying for advertising that doesn't work.

8 Branding

An aspect of marketing that is often overlooked is the idea of branding. While branding is related to marketing, it's not exactly the same thing as marketing. Marketing involves advertising your business, and branding is your business's image with the public. If you think of a company's 'brand name,' what sorts of things come to mind? The answers to that question are the characteristics that make up your company's brand.

Here are some questions to think about when creating a brand for your private practice:

What is your company's mission?
If you don't already have a mission statement for your private practice, you may want to take some time to compose one. A good mission statement should be less than one hundred words, but should be able to accurately reflect what your private practice is all about.

What are the benefits and features of your products or services?
What specialties do you offer that no other therapist in the area is offering? If your specialties are similar to those of other therapists and counselors in your town, what sets you apart from them? Why should a potential client choose you over your competitors? Do you have expertise in a particular diagnosis or a particular demographic? Do you have a therapy model that is rare or unique? What services do you offer that would attract potential clients to you above all others?

What do your customers and prospects think of your company?
If you've been in private practice for a while, it might be beneficial to give your customers a periodic survey to identify your strengths and your weaknesses as a therapist. Are your clients satisfied? What are potential areas for improvement? If you are a new private practice just starting out, you might post a survey on your website or by mail to test the waters and find out what your potential patients expect from your private practice once you get it up and running. It should be an ongoing part of your continuous improvement and quality control to ask for feedback on how you're doing in your given marketplace.

What qualities do you want the public to associate with your company?
What unique gifts do you bring to your practice of family therapy? Are any of these gifts marketable qualities? If you are patient and understanding with children, would you like them to associate those qualities with your private practice? If you have a special gift for teaching anger management, how would you express those talents to your public? Think about how you can turn your particular talents and skills into branding opportunities. How can you use your advertising campaign to present those characteristics to the public? The more you can talk about the unique qualities of your private practice, the more you create your own brand name.

What is your company's 'voice'?
Create a 'voice' for your company that reflects your brand. This voice should be applied to all written communication and incorporated in the visual imagery of all materials, online and off. Is your brand friendly? Be conversational. Is it ritzy? Be more formal. The idea is to use the tone and context of your private practice's printed communications to send a message to your public that tells them what you're all about. Develop a tagline that summarizes your company's voice. Write a memorable, meaningful and concise statement that captures the essence of your brand, and use it as often as possible. If your tagline or catchphrase is

short enough, you can even use it when you answer the telephone. Doing so builds brand recognition and automatically associates your private practice with your brand image.

What is your brand's message?
Write down your brand messaging. What are the key messages you want to communicate to the public, and therefore to potential clients, about your brand? For example, since my own business is centered on teaching mindfulness, I use a 'laid back' style and approach. Many people know me as 'that old hippy guy.' My brand's message is that if you seek me out for therapy you will enjoy a person-centered, calm and non-confrontational approach to therapy. Your approach will probably be somewhat different. Make sure your public knows exactly what to expect when they walk through your door.

If you have employees, every employee should be aware of your brand attributes to the point that they could summarize your private practice in two or three sentences at a cocktail party. You should be able to integrate your brand. Branding extends to every aspect of your business: How you answer your phones, what you wear on sales calls, your e-mail signature, the style and content of your advertising, and the décor of your office. Get a great logo. Place it everywhere. If you don't have the graphic design skills to come up with your own logo, hire a good graphic designer to create one for you. A great logo is recognizable even without explanatory text. Think about the Nike 'swoosh' or Disney's triple circle mouse head logo and you'll see what I mean. Those logos are instantly associated with their products without having to have the words 'Nike' or 'Disneyland' incorporated into the advertisement.

Once you have your logo and your tag line or catch phrase, design templates and create brand standards for your marketing materials. Use the same color scheme, logo placement, look and feel throughout all of your printed materials and online advertisements. You don't need to be fancy, just consistent. The idea here is to be able to build product recognition in your clients to the point that they automatically associate your logo and your tagline with you.

Can you be true to your brand?
Customers won't return to you, or refer someone else to you, if you don't deliver on your brand promise. Word-of-mouth advertising is probably the best form of advertising, and an unhappy customer can be highly detrimental to your business. If you brand yourself, for example, as a child-friendly therapist, but have difficulty in working with children's dynamics and special needs, your customers are going to notice the inconsistency between what your brand promises and what

you're able to deliver. If they're not happy with your services, they'll tell others. It is therefore imperative that your delivered services are always consistent with your branding message. If you cannot do this, your attempts at establishing a brand will fail.

Who should your 'branding' target?
At first glance, this question would seem to be asking who your ideal patient is, but the scope of your branding campaign is much wider than that. You are not only identifying the sort of people who would come to see you for therapy. You are also identifying the sort of people who might refer clients to you. The latter can sometimes be even more important. For example, if you specialize in Axis II disorders, and a doctor, psychiatrist or other therapist doesn't know that, and would like to refer a patient to someone, then you've just missed a valuable opportunity. When composing your branding package, be sure to include everyone for whom your branding message is intended.

Do you have a specialty skill?
A large part of your branding package will be about your specialty skills. If you are trained in Art Therapy, your branding should have an artistic feel. If you are trained in Music Therapy, your branding should reflect musical themes. If you are trained in Play Therapy, your branding should be attractive to children. Make a list of all the skills and training that make your private practice unique, and consider how your branding message will let the public know.

Do you have a specialty population?
If you are trained in Play Therapy, then at least one of your specialty populations is going to be children. If you are trained in marriage counseling, then one of your specialty populations is going to be married people (or at least couples). Think about the populations you'd like to work with, and then ask yourself what sorts of branding messages are likely to attract your specialty population to your practice. Once you have your answers, incorporate that information into your branding messages.

What is your key demographic?
Your key demographic is slightly different from your specialty population. While all members of your specialty population are contained within your key demographic, not all members of your key demographic are going to be a part of your specialty population. For example, suppose your specialty population is married people with

substance abuse disorders. You have two key demographics there: Married people, and people with substance abuse disorders. Your specialty population is where those two demographics overlap. In this instance, you will want some of your branding to focus on married people, and some of it to focus on people with substance abuse disorders. By casting a wider net, you are more likely to find people from your specific specialty population.

What are the likes and dislikes of your key demographic?
Once you have identified your key demographics, think about what they may like and what they may dislike. Try to avoid stereotypical thinking while doing this. Focus on commonsense associations. For example, if your key demographic is parent with small children, you probably already know that they will be interested in things like educational toys and children's books. So if you have these items in your waiting room, you're sending the message that you care about the comfort of your patients and that you want to accommodate them.

Who is your ideal client?
Think for a moment about your ideal client. What age group does your ideal client fall into? What is your ideal client's diagnosis? What is your ideal client's socio-economic status? What is the race, ethnicity, religion and sexual identity of your ideal client? What is the employment status of your ideal client? Take the answers to these questions and incorporate them into your branding message. For example, if you plan to work with LGBT-Q clients, you could offer links to resources and support groups on your website. If you plan to work with clients of a particular religious background, you could decorate your office with the iconography of that religion, or familiarize yourself with the nuances of belief of the various sects of that religion.

Why will your 'brand' appeal to your ideal client?
Put yourself in the shoes of your ideal client for a moment. Suppose you're looking for a therapist to meet your particular needs. What sort of brand message would you look for? Now take the answers to that question and incorporate them into your own brand message. The more effectively you can do this, the more likely you are to attract your ideal clients.

When is 'branding' effective?
You will know that your branding is effective when your customers have come to associate your private practice with a set of qualities that distinctively sets it apart from all other private practices in your region.

Branding gives your private practice a distinct identity. All of the components of branding, taken together, form the image of your business. Your brand is what your customers think of when they think of your business. Branding is your answer to the question, "Why should I choose you over every other business in town?" When your customers know the answer to that question, you will know that your branding is effective.

How should you brand your private practice?
Branding could best be summarized with the statement, "Stop telling me who you are and what you're going to do, and start telling me what you've already done!"
The idea here is that nothing succeeds like success. People are less interested in what you say you can do, and more interested in hearing what you've already done to help people. Keep track of your success stories so that potential clients can use that information to make informed decisions about hiring you to help them with their problems. Be aware that if you plan to use testimonials as a part of this 'success marketing' strategy, use extreme caution to make sure that your clients' confidentiality is not violated. *Always* have them sign a release of information if you plan to use quotes from former patients in your branding activities. If you are unsure of the limits of confidentiality in your state, check with your licensure board or your attorney.
At workshops and with individual and group therapy, keep outcome evaluations. I do an evaluation at intake, and then another at discharge. By scoring these evaluations, and comparing the numbers, you can chart improvement and adjust your services accordingly. Sometimes the fact that you do outcome evaluations is enough to let a patient know that you care about the quality of the services you're providing. And since the results of these outcome evaluations are numerical, without any identifying information, you can publish the statistics without violating the confidentiality of your clients. Even so, it's a good idea to have a statement in your intake paperwork asking permission to publish the results of these outcome evaluations. Include a space for comments, both positive and negative. You don't have to publish these comments. Use them to improve your services. If you intend to use the positive feedback in your branding materials, make sure you secure permission first.

What unique skills do you have as a therapist that could be incorporated into your branding message?
Do you have good listening skills? Therapists are trained to be good listeners, but you'd be surprised how many could actually benefit from

some help in this area. Are you really hearing what your patients are saying to you? Can you set aside your own therapy agenda and allow your patients to speak?

Do you have the ability to be in the moment with your patient? This means setting aside the treatment plans and goals for a moment when necessary so your patients can unpack. If you get too caught up in "what happens next," you can miss what your patients are saying to you in the moment.

Are you more of a Directive or Non-Directive therapist? Each approach has strengths and weaknesses, but try to avoid the trap of being *too* non-directive. Comedian Chris Titus tells of going to a therapist whose approach to therapy consisted mainly of asking the question, "And how did you feel about that?"

Chris's answer to this therapist was, "Ya know, Doc, for $300 an hour, I'd kind of like to know how *you* feel about that."

If you are a non-directive therapist, remember to occasionally check in with your patients to see if the approach is working for them. If this is your style, don't forget to mention it in your branding materials.

Are you naturally inquisitive? Do you truly want to know about your patients' lives and the solutions to their problems? If so, promote that aspect of your approach to therapy.

What are your 'growing edges'? Are there areas where you feel you could use a little more training or experience? You don't have to advertise your weaknesses in your branding materials, but if a client asks you about your skills in an area where you have little or no training, don't be afraid to tell them that you don't know. They'll appreciate your honesty much more than they would appreciate you attempting to provide services in an area with which you have no experience. Not only that, but if you attempt to provide services in an area for which you have not been trained, you are opening yourself up to lawsuits and ethical violations.

What are your natural areas of creativity? Could you incorporate those into your therapy somehow? Are you a musician? If so, have you considered training in music therapy? Are you an actor? Have you considered training in drama therapy? Your areas of creativity can be powerful branding tools that will set you apart from other private practices. Don't be afraid to use your interests in your branding materials.

What are your areas of flexibility? Can you be flexible in ways that would set you apart from other therapists? I see patients until 7 p.m., while many therapists in my city stop taking appointments at 5 p.m. This flexibility has allowed me to see people that other therapists would not. I have a friend who takes this to the extreme. He is a night owl. Because of this, he schedules his appointments from midnight until 8 a.m. His clients are mostly people who work third shift jobs. He does a lot of work specifically with night shift emergency room doctors and nurses using Trauma-Focused Cognitive Behavioral Therapy.

Think about the areas of flexibility that may set you apart from other therapists. Use your flexibility to your advantage, and incorporate it into your branding message.

When should you promote your brand?
The short answer to this question is 24 hours a day, seven days a week. To be really effective in branding and marketing, you should be thinking about branding and marketing opportunities from the time you wake up in the morning until the time you go to bed at night. Realistically speaking, there are some times that are more effective than others, depending on your key demographic. For example, if you work with children, summer is a great time to focus on branding your play therapy services, as most children are out of school. If you are an addiction specialist, focus your attention on branding more during holiday seasons, when people tend to indulge more.

Where should you promote your brand?
The short answer to this question is: Anywhere that works. This is where branding and marketing meet. When you have an opportunity to market your private practice, you also have an opportunity to brand your business. You can brand and market by leaving brochures and business cards at hospitals, treatment centers, day care centers, colleges, schools and non-profits. You also have the opportunity to be creative in your branding. Leaving brochures with your branding message at hospitals and treatment centers is a no-brainer, but have you thought about distributing them at spas, yoga classes, massage parlors, book stores, and coffee shops? Ask yourself where your target client or patient is likely to 'hang out,' then go there and leave brochures. (with permission from the owner, of course).

Branding Tips
The four key elements of branding are as follows:

Consistent Actions
Stay on-message with your branding, and deliver on your branding promises. If you state that you can do something in your marketing materials, make sure that you can do it.

Consistent Results
Use your outcome evaluations to make sure that you are delivering consistent services. If your outcome measures reveal any potential areas of inconsistency, address them as soon as possible so that you keep all of your clients satisfied.

Consistent Messages
As you develop your branding messages, you want to make sure that your various different messages don't conflict with each other. If you're branding yourself as an affordable therapist, and your fees are the highest in the region, your message isn't consistent. Periodically review how your brand is perceived in your local community and revise your messages as needed to maintain consistency.

Consistent Target Market
When you first start out in private practice, it's natural to try your hand with different populations and different markets until you find one that's a good fit. Eventually you're going to want to settle on an area of expertise. Once you do that, you're going to want to consistently pursue that market. For example, when I first started out I wanted to work with children and to develop my play therapy skills. The more I got into this market, the more I started getting high-conflict divorce cases that were less about therapy for the children and more about attorneys gaining evidence for custody disputes than about therapy for the children. So I switched my focus to marital counseling. It took almost a year to stop getting referrals for therapy with children. Fortunately my partner at the time did play therapy, or I may have alienated potential future clients.
Once you've settled on a market, make sure to stick with it, or if you have to transition, plan ahead so that the transition is a smooth one.

A great way to begin your branding campaign is to build your social network. Get in touch with old friends and tell them what you're planning to do. You may also ask them what they think your strengths and weaknesses are, and how you might incorporate them into building a brand.

Pursue interests and activities that mean a lot to you. Look for ways to blend these activities into your branding. Do you enjoy knitting? Maybe you could start a 'knitting therapy' group. How about windsurfing, or bicycling? Could you host groups that engage in these activities for therapeutic purposes? Virtually any hobby has a therapeutic aspect, or people probably wouldn't engage in such activities in the first place.

Another way to get ideas for your branding campaign is to go to work-related conferences and see how others in the profession are branding themselves. What stands out? Which branding ideas could you use for your own business? Go to conferences likely to attract your key demographic so that you will have a better understanding of how to market to that demographic.

When you're at conferences and other events, find out who knows whom, and keep track of these connections. Make a flow chart if needed. Keep a notebook or database for referral purposes. If you refer to people with areas of expertise outside of your own, then others are more likely to refer clients to you for your areas of expertise.

A great way to find events to attend for purposes of networking is to obtain a list of the non-profits in your area, visit their websites, and look at their event schedules. It would be even better if you could go introduce yourself personally, and give them some brochures and business cards. A great place to get a list of non-profits in your area is the United Way Directory at www.unitedway.org.

As new people move into the area, and as new colleagues get credentialed, get to know them. Introduce yourself, tell them your areas of expertise, and ask for theirs. Use this information to cross-refer to each other. As your network grows, invite people out to lunch or coffee on a periodic basis to touch bases and inform each other of new developments with your practices. Attend events, and sponsor events. Get involved in causes related to your specialty. If you are an advocate for LGBT-Q rights and related therapeutic issues, get involved with Parents and Friends of Lesbians and Gays (PFLAG). If you specialize in working with senior citizens, get involved with the Alzheimer's Association. If you work with families, why not volunteer with the National Alliance on Mental Illness (NAMI)? Whatever your specialty, there is probably a related organization. Networking with these organizations allows you the opportunity to tell them about your brand and your services, and it also allows you to give back to the community.

Follow Up

As you continue to build brand awareness by networking with other professionals, and with laypeople, it is important to follow up with them on occasion so that your brand stays fresh on their minds. Call all your contacts at least once every six months for coffee or another get-together. Send 'thank you' notes when they refer to you. You don't have to do this for every referral, but it's nice to get a periodic reminder that you appreciate their referrals. Send holiday cards and let them know they're on your mind. Above all, refer to others so that they will be more likely to refer to you. The ultimate in branding is to brand your private practice as a team player within your local and regional mental health communities.

AFTERWORD

Going into private practice will be one of the most rewarding, and frustrating, experiences of your life. If you are in the mental health field, it's the greatest opportunity to help people without agency restrictions on the types of therapy you do, and how you do it. It's why you got into a helping profession in the first place.

Although the first year of private practice will be a confusing whirlwind of paperwork, marketing, government regulations, insurance regulations, and number-crunching, if you survive your first year private practice will offer you a flexibility and freedom not found in the 9 to 5 world.

If you've read this book, you have a good basic grasp of what it will take. Now comes the work of investigating everything it would take to make your dream happen. Appendix A contains a list of Private Practice Resources to help you investigate what it would take to open a private practice within your particular area of expertise and within your geographical location. Appendix B is a Private Practice Checklist that will guide you through the steps required to open your business. Appendix C is a list of addresses and contact information for the Secretaries of State in the United States. You would need to contact them for information on incorporating your business or non-profit. The References section contains suggestions for further reading before setting out on the adventure that is private practice.

If a private practice is your dream, you now have the basic tools needed to begin. Good luck, and have a happy journey!

Appendix A: Private Practice Resources

American Art Therapy Association
National Office
American Art Therapy Association
4875 Eisenhower Avenue, Suite 240
Alexandria VA 22304
888-290-0878
703-548-5860
703-783-8468 (FAX)
http://www.arttherapy.org

American Association of Sexuality Educators, Counselors and Therapists (AASECT)
AASECT
444 I Street, NW, Suite 700
Washington DC 20005
Telephone (202) 449-1099
Fax (202) 216-9646
info@aasect.org
http://www.aasect.org

American Counseling Association
5999 Stevenson Ave.
Alexandria, VA 22304
ACA Fax Number: (703) 823-0252
ACA Toll-Free Numbers: ACA: (800) 347-6647
FAX: (800) 473-2329

American Dance Therapy Association
0632 Little Patuxent Parkway
Suite 108
Columbia MD 21044
PHONE: 410-997-4040
FAX: 410-997-4048
Or visit http://www.adta.org

American Music Therapy Association
American Music Therapy Association
8455 Colesville Road, Suite 1000,
Silver Spring MD 20910
Phone: 301.589.3300

Fax: 301.589.5175
http://www.musictherapy.org

American Psychological Association
750 First St. NE, Washington, DC 20002-4242
Telephone: (800) 374-2721
(202) 336-5500
TDD/TTY: (202) 336-6123
http://www.apa.org

Association for Play Therapy
Association for Play Therapy, Inc.
3198 Willow Avenue
Suite 110
Clovis CA 93612
Telephone: 559·294·2128
Fax: 559·294·2129
E·mail: info@a4pt.org
http://www.a4pt.org

Employee Assistance Program Association
4350 North Fairfax Drive, Suite 740
Arlington, Virginia 22203 U.S.A.
Phone: 703-387-1000
Fax: 703-522-4585
http://www.eapassn.org

Employee Assistance Society of North America (EASNA)
The Value of Employee Assistance Programs, (2009), http://www.easna.org.

Internal Revenue Service
http://www.irs.gov

International Coach Federation (ICF)
2365 Harrodsburg Rd
Suite A325
Lexington KY 40504
888.423-3131
1-859-219-3580
Fax: (859) 226-4411
Email: icfheadquarters@coachfederation.org
http://www.coachfederation.org

Mindfulness-Based Family Therapy
Training and continuing education for therapists, counselors and other mental health professionals
http://www.mbft.org

National Association of Alcohol and Drug Abuse Counselors (NAADAC)
1001 N. Fairfax St. Suite 201
Alexandria VA 22314
Telephone (703) 741-7686 or (800) 548-0497
Fax (703) 741-7698 or (800) 377-1136
Email naadac@naadac.org

National Association of Social Workers
750 First Street, NE
Suite 700
Washington, DC 20002-4241
membership@naswdc.org
Telephone (800) 742-4089

National Council of Nonprofits
Information on starting up a nonprofit, as well as listings of nonprofits throughout the United States
National Council of Nonprofits
1200 New York Avenue, NW
Suite 700 Washington, DC 20005
P: (202) 962-0322 | F: (202) 962-0321
http://www.councilofnonprofits.org

North American Drama Therapy Association
44365 Premier Plaza, Suite 220
Ashburn, VA 20147
(888) 416-7167
(703) 738-7065
office@nadt.org
http://www.nadt.org

Appendix B: Private Practice Checklist

- ☐ Do a Cost/Benefit Analysis to see if I am ready to start a private practice
- ☐ Do a strengths and weaknesses inventory to see what areas I might need help with
- ☐ Start a list of resources for getting help in those areas
- ☐ Decide on a name for the business
- ☐ Find a location for the business
- ☐ Check to see if the location is handicapped accessible
- ☐ If it is not, check to see if local laws require therapy offices to be handicapped accessible
- ☐ Decide on a type and structure for my business entity
- ☐ Get legal assistance if necessary to determine the proper type of business entity for my private practice
- ☐ File proper paperwork to register my private practice
- ☐ Get a National Provider Identification (NPI) number
- ☐ Get a Federal Employer Identification Number (FEIN)
- ☐ Open a DBA business account
- ☐ Get all necessary business licenses and permits
- ☐ Introduce myself to the local Chamber of Commerce and/or Small Business Associations
- ☐ Get liability insurance for malpractice
- ☐ Get liability 'slip and fall' policy
- ☐ Get accounting software
- ☐ Buy office furniture
- ☐ Buy office supplies
- ☐ Hire an accountant or learn accounting for private practice
- ☐ Set up a bookkeeping system
- ☐ Create a business plan
- ☐ Create a projected profit and loss statement for at least three years
- ☐ Register to pay estimated taxes
- ☐ Apply to an insurance panel that uses CAQH to verify credentials
- ☐ Create a CAQH account
- ☐ Use CAQH credentialing to apply for more insurance panels, EAPs and HMOs
- ☐ If planning to accept Medicaid and/or Medicare, begin the process of applying
- ☐ If necessary, take a class on insurance billing if I plan to do my own billing, or hire a medical coding agency to do my billing for me
- ☐ Obtain insurance billing software if needed

- ☐ Investigate the Certified Employee Assistance Professional (CEAP®) Credential and apply if interested
- ☐ Join my local professional organization (American Association of Marriage and Family Therapists, et al)
- ☐ Investigate membership in other related professional organizations
- ☐ Decide on an advertising campaign
- ☐ Design business cards and have them printed
- ☐ Design brochures and have them printed
- ☐ Target different brochures for different situations/agencies
- ☐ Begin to build a branding message and a branding campaign
- ☐ Begin networking by visiting local referral sources in the area (doctors, non-profit agencies, treatment centers, etc.)
- ☐ Open the doors and begin taking appointments!

Appendix C: Secretaries of State

NOTE: In the states of Alaska, Hawaii, and Utah, there is no Secretary of State, therefore contact information for these states will not be listed below. In those states many duties of a Secretary of State fall within the domain of the Lieutenant Governor.

Alabama
EXECUTIVE DIVISION
State Capitol Building - Suite S-105
600 Dexter Avenue
Phone: 334-242-7200   Fax: 334-242-4993

Arizona
Secretary of State
1700 W. Washington Street, Fl. 7
Phoenix, AZ 85007-2808

Arkansas
Business Office
Phone: 501-682-8032

California
Certification and Records
P.O. Box 944260
Sacramento, CA 94244–2600

Colorado
Colorado Department of State
1700 Broadway
Denver, CO 80290
303-894-2200

Connecticut
Office of the Secretary of the State
State of Connecticut
30 Trinity Street
Hartford, CT 06106
Telephone: (860) 509-6200

Delaware
Division of Corporations
John G. Townsend Building
401 Federal Street - Suite 4
Dover, DE 19901

Florida
Telephone 850.245.6500
Fax 850.245.6125
TDD Line 850.245.6096
Florida Relay Service (TDD)   800.955.8771

Georgia
2 MLK Jr. Dr. S.E.
Suite 315, Floyd West Tower
Atlanta, Georgia 30334
Telephone: 404-656-2817
FAX: 404-657-6380

Idaho
Idaho Secretary of State's Office
Attn: Business Entities Division
PO Box 83720
Boise ID 83720-0080
Phone: 1(208) 334-2301
Fax: 1(208) 334-2080
Website: www.sos.idaho.gov/corp/corindex.htm
E-Mail: sosinfo@sos.idaho.gov

Illinois
800-252-8980 (toll free in Illinois)
213 State Capitol
Springfield, IL 62756
217-785-3000 (outside Illinois)

Indiana
Office of the Indiana Secretary of State
200 W. Washington St., Room 201
Indianapolis, IN 46204
Phone: 317-232-6531
FAX: 317-233-3283

Iowa
Secretary of State
First Floor, Lucas Building
321 E. 12th St.
Des Moines, IA 50319
sos@sos.iowa.gov
(515) 281-5204

Kansas
Kansas Secretary of State
Memorial Hall, 1st Floor
120 SW 10th Avenue
Topeka, KS 66612-1594
(785) 296-4564

Kentucky
Kentucky Secretary of State
700 Capital Ave., Ste. 152
Frankfort, KY 40601
P: (502) 564-3490
F: (502) 564-5687

Louisiana
Corporations
Phone: 225.925.4704
Fax: 225.932.5314
Legal Services
Phone: 225.925.4704
Fax: (225) 932-5317

Maine
Office of the Secretary
Matthew Dunlap
148 State House Station
Augusta, Maine 04333-0148
Tel: 207-626-8400
Fax: 207-287-8598

Maryland
16 Francis Street
Annapolis, MD 21401
Phone: 410-974-5521
FAX: 410-974-5190

Massachusetts
Secretary of the Commonwealth
Corporations Division
McCormack Building
One Ashburton Place, 17th floor
Boston, MA 02108
Phone: 617-727-9640
Fax: 617-742-4538

Michigan
Michigan Department of State
Lansing, MI 48918
 (888) SOS-MICH

Minnesota
Retirement Systems of Minnesota Building
60 Empire Dr., Suite 100
Saint Paul, MN 55103
651-296-2803

Mississippi
700 North Street
Jackson, MS 39202
(601) 359-1633

Missouri
600 West Main Street
Jefferson City, MO 65101
Main Office: (573) 751-4936

Montana
Montana Secretary of State's Office
P.O. Box 202801
Helena, MT 59620
Phone: (406) 444-2034
Fax: (406) 444-3976

Nebraska
P.O. Box 94608
Lincoln, NE 68509-4608
Phone: (402) 471-2554
Fax: (402) 471-3237

Nevada
Secretary of State
Nevada State Capitol Building
101 North Carson Street, Suite 3
Carson City, NV 89701
Phone: 775-684-5708
FAX: 775-684-5725
Email: sosmail@sos.nv.gov

New Hampshire
Corporation Division
N.H. Department of State
107 North Main Street
Concord, NH 03301-4989
603-271-3246

New Jersey
New Jersey Department of State
225 W.State Street
P.O. Box 300
Trenton, NJ 08625
Email: Feedback@sos.state.nj.us

New Mexico
New Mexico Capitol Annex North
325 Don Gaspar, Suite 300
Santa Fe, NM 87501
505.827.4508

New York
New York State, Department of State
Division of Corporations, State Records
and Uniform Commercial Code
99 Washington Avenue 6th floor
Albany, NY 12231
Corporations Information: (518) 473-2492

North Carolina
NC Secretary of State
PO Box 29622
Raleigh NC 27626-0622

North Dakota
Secretary of State
State of North Dakota
600 E Boulevard Avenue Dept 108
Bismarck ND 58505-0500
Telephone: 701-328-2900
Toll Free: 800-352-0867
TTY: 800-366-6888
Fax: 701-328-2992
Email: sos@nd.gov

Ohio
180 East Broad Street, 16th Floor
Columbus, Ohio 43215
(614) 466-2655
(877) SOS-Ohio (767-6446)

Oklahoma
Secretary of State
2300 N. Lincoln Boulevard, Ste. 101
Oklahoma City, OK 73105-4897
(405) 521-3912

Oregon
Corporation Division
Public Service Building Suite 151
255 Capitol Street NE
Salem OR 97310
phone (503) 986-2200

Pennsylvania
Department of State
401 North Street
Room 206
Harrisburg, PA 17120
Phone:(717) 787-1057
Phone:(888) 659-9962

Rhode Island
148 West River Street
Providence, RI 02904-2615
Phone: (401) 222-3040
Fax: (401) 222-1309

South Carolina
SC Secretary of State's Office
1205 Pendleton Street Suite 525
Columbia, SC 29201

South Dakota
500 E Capitol Ave #204
Pierre, SD 57501
(605) 773-3537

Tennessee
312 Rosa L. Parks Avenue
6th Floor, Snodgrass Tower
Nashville, TN 37243-1102
Phone: (615) 741-2286

Texas
Corporations Section
P.O. Box 13697
Austin, Texas 78711-3697

Vermont
Secretary's Office
128 State Street
Montpelier, VT 05633-1101
802-828-2363
800-439-8683
802-828-2496 FAX

Virginia
Office of the Secretary of the Commonwealth
P.O. Box 2454
Richmond, VA 23218
(804) 786-2441
Fax: (804) 371-0017

Washington
Washington Secretary of State
Legislative Building
PO Box 40220
Olympia, WA 98504-0220
Telephone: (360) 902-4151
Business Services: (360) 725-0377

West Virginia
Secretary of State
Bldg. 1, Suite 157-K
1900 Kanawha Blvd. East
Charleston, WV 25305-0770
Business and Licensing (304) 558-8000
Toll-Free (866) 767-8683
Fax Number: (304) 558-0900

Wisconsin
Office of the Secretary
P.O. Box 7848
Madison, WI 53707-7848
Email: statesec@sos.state.wi.us
608-266-8888
FAX: 608-266-3159

Wyoming
Wyoming Secretary of State's Office
State Capitol Building
200 West 24th Street
Cheyenne, WY 82002-0020
Ph. 307.777.7378
Fax 307.777.6217
secofstate@wyo.gov

References

Bazelon, David L. (2010). *How Will Health Reform Help People with Mental Illnesses? An analysis of the Affordable Care Act passed by Congress in 2010 and how it will affect people with psychiatric disabilities.* Bazelon Center for Mental Health Law, 1101 Fifteenth Street NW, Suite 1212, Washington DC 20005.

Cyboran, S.F., & Donahue, R., (2007). How to Improve the Behavioral Health of an Organization, *Perspectives 15(3),* (The Segal Group, Inc., October 2007), www.sibson.com/publications/perspectives/volume_15_issue_3/behavioral_health.html.

Employee Assistance Program Association, http://www.eapassn.org

Employee Assistance Society of North America (EASNA), *The Value of Employee Assistance Programs,* (2009), http://www.easna.org.

Finch, R.A., & Phillips, K., Center for Prevention and Health Services, *An Employer's Guide to Behavioral Health Services: A Roadmap and Recommendations for Evaluating, Designing, and Implementing Behavioral Health Services,* (Washington, DC: National Business Group on Health, 2005).

Fogarty, S., (2006). Comorbidity Addressed Effectively via an Integrated Solution, *Compensation & Benefits Review 38(5).*

Hargrave, G.E., & Hiatt, D. (2007). The EAP Treatment of Depressed Employees: Implications for Return on Investment, *Managed Health Network.*

H. Harwood, D. Fountain, & G. Livermore, The Economic Costs of Alcohol & Drug Abuse in the U.S. 1992. Rockville, MD: *National Institute on Drug Abuse and National Institute on Alcohol Abuse and Alcoholism, 1998.* http://www. nida.nih.gov/economiccosts/index.html . (Accessed 5-9-08)

International Coach Federation (ICF), http://www.coachfederation.org

Langlieb, A.M., & Kahn, J.P., (2005). How Much Does Quality Mental Health Care Profit Employers? *Journal of Occupational and Environmental Medicine 47(11), (2005).*

Larson, S.L. Eyerman, J., Foster, M.S., and Gfroerer, J.C. (2007). *Worker*

Substance Use and Workplace Policies and Programs. Rockville, MD: SAMHSA, OAS, 2007. http://www.oas.samhsa.gov/work2k7/work.htm#6.1 . (Accessed 5-16-08).

Musich, D. Napier and D.W. Edington, "The Association of Health Risks with Worker's Compensations Costs," *Journal of Occupational and Environmental Medicine*. 43, 6: 534-541 (June 2001).

National Institute of Mental Health, (revised 2008). *Depression. (National Institutes of Health publication No. 08 3561)*.

National Institute on Drug Abuse, Principles of Drug Addiction Treatment: A Research-Based Guide, FAQ11. Bethesda, MD, 1999. http://www.nida.nih.gov/ podat/PODAT6.html#FAQ11 . (Accessed 5-9-08).

New Freedom Commission on Mental Health, *Achieving the Promise: Transforming Mental Health Care in America*. (2003).

Partnership for Workplace Mental Health, *A Mentally Healthy Workforce: It's Good for Business*, (2006), www.workplacementalhealth.org.

Partnership for Workplace Mental Health, *Successful Employer Implementation of the Federal Mental Health Parity and Addiction Equity Act, Research Works 1(3), (December 2009)*, www.workplacementalhealth.org/researchworks.aspx

Pilette, P.C., (2005). Presenteeism & Productivity: Two Reasons Employee Assistance Programs Make Good Business Cents, *Annals of the American Psychotherapy Association 8, (2005)*.

SAMHSA, Office of Applied Studies, *National Survey on Drug Use and Health 2005 and 2006: Table 5.8A*. Rockville, MD, 2007. http://oas.samhsa.gov/nsduh2k6nsduh/tabs/Sect5peTabs1to13.pdf. (Accessed 5-7-08).

Schneider Institute for Health Policy, Brandeis University, *Substance Abuse, The Nation's Number One Health Problem*, Princeton, NJ: Robert Wood Johnson Foundation, February 2001:70.

Sederer, L.I., & Clemens, N.A., (2002). The Business Case for High-Quality Mental Health Care, *Psychiatric Services 53(2)*.

Stewart, W.F., Ricci, J.A., Chee, E., et al., (2003). Cost of Lost Productive

Work Time among U.S. Workers with Depression, *Journal of the American Medical Association 289(23), (2003)*.

ABOUT Charlton Hall, MMFT, LMFT

Charlton Hall, MMFT, LMFT is a licensed Marriage and Family Therapist. He has a background as an Addictions Counselor, and worked in that capacity for several years prior to becoming a Marriage and Family Therapist. He is the owner of a successful private practice in Greenville, South Carolina, and he provides continuing education trainings for therapists and other mental health professionals. Prior to becoming a therapist, he was a small business owner for over two decades.
You may reach him at chuck@mbft.org
Visit his website at www.mbft.org

OTHER BOOKS BY CHARLTON HALL

The Mindful Ecotherapy Handbook combines the skills of Mindfulness and the healing power of nature found in Ecotherapy into a coherent framework to facilitate wellbeing and personal growth. By using nature and living in the present moment, readers of this book will achieve new levels of self-awareness, relaxation and self-confidence.
ISBN-10: 1482035847
ISBN-13: 978-1482035841

Green Circles: A Sustainable Journey from the Cradle to the Grave offers a unique perspective on green living by observing environmentally friendly living throughout the human life cycle. Starting with natural childbirth, finishing with green burial, and examining all phases of life in-between, Hall offers tips and suggestions to help each of us live a greener lifestyle.
ISBN-10: 1481977733
ISBN-13: 978-1481977739

The 7Cs of Mindful Mood Management Workbook is a resource book for those dealing with problems of emotional aggression and emotional addiction. Although it was designed to be used in conjunction with the 12-week Mindful Mood Management program, it may also be useful as a reference for those who have difficulty with emotional regulation.
DUE TO BE RELEASED IN SPRING OF 2014

www.ingramcontent.com/pod-product-compliance
Lightning Source LLC
Chambersburg PA
CBHW051215170526
45166CB00005B/1913